GREEN MADE EASY

Hay House Titles of Related interest

GREEN MADE EASY

The EVERYDAY GUIDE for Transitioning to a Green Lifestyle

CHRIS PRELITZ

HAY HOUSE, INC.
Carlsbad, California • New York City
London • Sydney • Johannesburg
Vancouver • Hong Kong • New Delhi

Published and distributed in the United States by: Hay House, Inc.: www.hayhouse.com • *Published and distributed in Australia by:* Hay House Australia Pty. Ltd.: www.hayhouse.com.au • *Published and distributed in the United Kingdom by:* Hay House UK, Ltd.: www.hay house.co.uk • *Published and distributed in the Republic of South Africa by:* Hay House SA (Pty), Ltd.: www.hayhouse.co.za • *Distributed in Canada by:* Raincoast: www.raincoast.com • *Published in India by:* Hay House Publishers India: www.hayhouse.co.in

Editorial supervision: Jill Kramer • *Design:* Amy Rose Grigoriou
Interior illustrations: Gregory Grigoriou

Library of Congress Cataloging-in-Publication Data

Prelitz, Chris
  Green made easy : the everyday guide for transitioning to a green lifestyle / Chris Prelitz. -- 1st ed.
    p. cm.
  ISBN 978-1-4019-2284-9 (tradepaper : alk. paper) 1. Environmental responsibility. 2. Sustainable living. 3. Green products. I. Title.
  GE195.7.P74 2009
  640--dc22

                                        2008032001

ISBN: 978-1-4019-2284-9

12 11 10 09   4 3 2 1
1st edition, April 2009

Printed in the United States of America

For generations to come

CONTENTS

PREFACE

Today, my wife, Becky, and I live in a solar-powered green home just a short walk from the ocean in Laguna Beach, California. Most months we get a credit from our power company instead of a bill. Our solar-electric panels make more energy than we use, including enough to power the little electric GEM car that serves as our daily driver around town. We pick fresh vegetables and fruit from our edible forest garden that covers more than half of our lot. Our home has been featured on television and in a half-dozen magazines. Calls are coming in with requests for us to consult with certain cities, or companies such as Mercedes-Benz, as well as to deliver keynote addresses on our energy future, green business opportunities, or green building methods. A green home flip we completed and sold was documented on the Discovery Channel's Planet Green TV show *Greenovate*.

When we feel the need to get away to a quieter spot, we drive out and stay at our off-grid solar-powered retreat cabin, nestled on 40 acres of pristine wilderness near Taos, New Mexico. I feel so grateful for all of the blessings and abundance in my life. But it wasn't always this way. A dozen short years ago, life was very, very different for me.

I've always been passionate about the environment. In 1992, I learned that rice straw was typically burned after the harvest, and the black soot rising from the rice fields was the number one cause of air pollution in California. To combat this, two friends and I founded the nonprofit organization CASBA (California Straw Building Association) with the goal of making straw-bale construction code-approved in California. This would provide a market for the rice straw and create an annually renewable construction material with incredibly high insulation value. CASBA was instrumental in acquiring the fire, moisture, and load testing that allowed straw-bale construction to become code-legal. I also served on the board of directors of another nonprofit, the Eos Institute, which published *Earthword,* one of the first journals on sustainability. This was all wonderfully rewarding work, but none of it payed the rent very well.

Come 1996, I was doing whatever green design or construction projects I could find, but those were few and far between. I was considered, shall we say, a little "out there" by most folks back then. Even though I had built the first permitted solar-powered home in our county for some clients two years earlier, there still wasn't much demand or awareness for anything green. Gasoline was $1.30 a gallon, and the economy was, as one financial magazine reported, "as good or better than *the good old days.*"

Heidi, my first wife, and I were renting a small house that didn't even have a working furnace. We would burn scrounged wood in the fireplace to stay warm in winter. We just couldn't manage to save up enough money for the down payment on a house. Our landlord at the time was starting to be a bit of a challenge, so Heidi and I decided to look for another house to rent. It wasn't easy finding a place that would allow us to have three pets: our golden retriever, Jeremy; and two cats, Misha and Irie.

One day while we were out searching, we stumbled across a vacant dirt lot that had just come up for sale. It was at the bottom of a quiet canyon but had a number of issues. It was basically a big funnel-shaped hole in the ground with power lines and a watercourse running through it. And at the very bottom of the hole was a huge metal drainpipe. Almost everyone would say that the lot was pretty ugly, but when I walked around the property for the first time, a vision of a home came into my mind. I felt like it could really work for us. And most important, I could face the home southward so it looked down the canyon.

We used a credit card for the initial down payment and prayed that everything would work out for financing. And it did. I spent the next few months with late nights and little sleep, designing a home that could meet our needs and fit into the small sliver of high ground next to the watercourse. I designed a two-story straw-bale and wood-frame home with a day-lit basement, very similar to the one in my grandfather's passive solar home back in Illinois. (My family would visit our grandparents in the summertime, and no matter how hot it was outside, it would always be cool and comfortable downstairs in the day-lit basement connected to the cool of the earth.)

Heidi and I planted the gardens first so we'd have a view of lush foliage instead of barren dirt when we moved in. In addition, landscaping where we weren't going to build would give the new plants almost two years to grow and fill in. Our vision was to transform the bowl-shaped lot into stone paths, streambeds, and gardens with fruit trees. There would be no grass lawn. I vowed that I'd never mow a lawn again after all the years behind a push mower as a kid. We broke ground in June 1998 and were ecstatic at finally being able to design and build our dream home together.

By April 1999, the home was about halfway built, when Heidi woke up one morning and said she'd had a very powerful dream the night before. It was strikingly vivid, as if it were in Technicolor. She was walking alongside a river when a large white snake rose up in front of her. She looked eye to eye with the snake for quite some time. Heidi, when recounting the dream, told me that she didn't feel afraid at all. Then without warning, the snake bit her on the chest. She said that she felt like she was dying in the dream, and it was very peaceful. Next, she saw our Native American friend from New Mexico, Thomas One Wolf, rowing a bright white canoe across the river to take her to the other side. That's when she woke up.

That morning we talked for some time about what the symbolism of her dream might mean, about death, and what we'd do if we lost each other. I'll always remember Heidi's words: "If something ever happens to me, find someone great and love her, because love is all that matters." I agreed and asked her to do the same. A week later, Heidi suffered a fatal heart attack. She was 42.

Words poorly express the emotions I went through over the weeks and months that followed. I came so close to running away, but many dear friends supported me through the anger, sadness, grief, and loss. Completing the home became my therapy. I knew it was what Heidi would have wanted.

One of the most difficult things to deal with when you lose someone is the constant reminder that would come in the mail every day. I asked at the post office about somehow stopping her mail, but they said there was nothing they could do. I'm sure I bent the law, but I saw no other way out: I filed a change of address for Heidi to her last place of residence—the local coroner's office. It worked, and all of her mail stopped. After about a year, with a lot of support from friends, the home was complete enough to pass final inspection.

Around that time, an invitation for a Chicago seminar with spiritual teacher Ron Roth arrived in the mail, addressed to Heidi. It was the only letter for Heidi I'd received since filing the change of address, and I inexplicably felt drawn to go. During the three-day event, I introduced myself to a woman wearing a name tag that said she was also from Laguna Beach. "No, they made a mistake on the name tag," she said. "I'm from Long Beach" (another community on the Southern California coast). Becky and I felt an instant connection, and I invited her to visit when she returned to California. When Becky entered the Laguna Beach house, it took her breath away, and she started to cry. She shared with me that five years earlier, she had dreamed about living in a home very much like the one I'd built.

Becky and I began dating, and we finished the interior of the home together. In March 2001, in the shade of fruit trees and surrounded by native flowers and fragrant herbs, we planted a wedding tree as friends gathered to celebrate our union on the sacred ground of our garden. We often say that we have an arranged marriage, made in heaven.

THE BIG GREEN PICTURE

From actors to oil companies, everyone is jumping on the green bandwagon. *Green* has emerged as the new buzzword for hip, cool, and socially responsible. It is also an unstoppable movement toward an elevated consciousness and a different way of living. Most of us would agree that we thrive on clean air, clean water, and healthy food. The question we're facing is how we can be the best stewards of those gifts and resources while ensuring that future generations will enjoy them as well.

We're discovering that going green makes sense for the environment and improves our health and well-being. We're discovering that as we evolve spiritually, our preferences also evolve. And we're discovering new and better methods for providing for our needs, along with rediscovering ancient principles that our ancestors developed and refined over centuries. Surprisingly, many are realizing that going green in their lifestyle is also making them greener financially.

Mega companies not typically known for their social or environmental record, such as DuPont, BP, Walmart, and Target, are going green because it makes bottom-line dollar sense. They have all experienced huge financial gains through energy saving and green technologies. Target retail stores have installed solar panels on the roofs of many of their buildings, offsetting 20 percent of those stores' annual energy costs. Walmart installed plastic balers in its stores and now makes an additional $28 million a year by recycling and selling the plastic that it used to throw away.

As Walmart CEO Lee Scott said, "Think about it. If we throw it away, we had to buy it first. So we pay twice—once to get it, once to have it taken away. What if we reverse that? What if our suppliers send us less, and everything they send us has value as a recycled product? No waste, and we get paid instead." I would encourage Mr. Scott to continue in that direction and suggest, as another cost-efficient step, that he look at sourcing more products from this side of the Pacific Ocean. Many companies are implementing policies that are truly making a difference, and they're learning that sustainable solutions that are safer for consumers are also healthier for their workers, are cutting insurance costs, and often are more profitable.

Unfortunately, some companies are *greenwashing*—spending more money on their green advertising than on environmentally friendly practices. Walk the aisles of most retail stores and you'll be overwhelmed by all the marketing claims of "clean," "green," "environmentally friendly," or "natural." Everything on Earth is part of nature or "natural," but do consumers really want natural toxins such as lead in their lipstick or mercury in their mascara? Coal is natural, and it's now being marketed as a "clean fuel," even though coal-burning power plants are some of the worst offenders of pollution on the planet. Other products state totally irrelevant claims such as "CFC free," even though CFCs (chlorofluorocarbons) were banned more than 20 years ago. Bamboo floors are all the rage, with bamboo being marketed as an annually renewable crop. But advertisers don't mention that nearly all of it comes from the Far East, and immense amounts of fuel are used for transporting it from there to here.

With so many options, it can be overwhelming to figure out who's giving the straight scoop and which products or services are just using greenwashing to lure in the consumer. Here's my simple take on what the green movement is:

Going green is about making different choices—choices that are healthier and create greater joy for every living being, and that will sustain a better planet for generations to come.

Now, more than ever before, it's imperative for us to experience and express gratitude for the abundance and life-giving nurturing that our planet provides us each day. We must awaken to a deeper understanding that each of us influences and adds to the design and tapestry of our life. We have a window of opportunity to be important agents for change. Through the rapid dissemination of information over the Internet, we now can witness with an unprecedented reality our civilization's impact on the life-support systems of the earth. Most of our natural systems from oceans and rivers to rainforests and grasslands are in need of healing, repair, and restoration. Our industrial thoughtlessness has poisoned the air, water, and soil. Our practice of extracting resources for onetime disposable use is needlessly wasteful. It took nature 100 million years to create the energy the world uses today in one year.[1] Asthma, cancer, and many other diseases are more prevalent than at any time in recorded history.

We have the opportunity to become better stewards of Mother Earth by rethinking, retooling, and redoing the way we use and reuse resources. With each dollar we spend as consumers, we can support businesses, farmers, and corporations that are conscious of the global impact of their operations, that make better choices, and that will emerge as leaders in the green movement, which is unfolding at unprecedented speed.

With awareness, we can make simple but different choices that are safer for our bodies, our children, and our world—many of which are offered in this book. They can help dramatically improve our personal health and our ecosystems while ensuring that future generations will also have the ability to thrive on this magnificent planet.

ABOUT
GREEN MADE EASY

My heart's desire is that this book will help you on your path toward making choices you feel great about— those that have a lighter impact on the planet, are better for every living thing, and which will ultimately save you money in the long run. It would take a set of encyclopedias to address every consumer option available, so I've included items that make the biggest difference for your personal health and wellbeing, as well as for the environment.

This book is divided into three parts. "Green Your Life" covers choices for personal care, food, kids, and pets. "Green Your Home" teaches you ways to create a bedroom sanctuary (and why that's so important in our toxin-filled world), as well as providing helpful information on everything from water and recycling to selecting green cleaning supplies and furnishings. The last section, "More Green for Home, Work, and Play," finishes up with green options for lighting, electronics, and appliances, in addition to offering green tips for the workplace and when traveling.

Each chapter begins with a story. Many are from my own walk down the green path of life. Some are from two decades ago when I was single, others are from when I was married to Heidi, and some are more recent events that Becky and I have shared together. The stories were chosen to support the subject of the chapter, and they aren't necessarily written down in consecutive order. I've added details to each that will help you understand where I was in my life's walk at that point. I've also included anecdotes I've found interesting or relevant, which help illustrate the chapter's theme. These narratives are followed by easy action steps and brief descriptions that show the impact or importance of each choice.

I've basically distilled my 20-plus years of experience—trial and error, mistakes and successes —into an easy-to-use guide filled with eco-choices that I know work. This book will continue to serve as a handy reference guide long after you've gone through it from cover to cover. It's full of research and Websites that I still refer to when I need more information. You may also learn things you never knew, such as what EMFs (electromagnetic fields) are or what powers vampires are, and how to stop them.

The more green choices you make, the easier it gets. And as you discover the benefits of a healthier home or workplace and experience the physical, financial, and spiritual rewards, you'll want to go further and further down the green road. One day you'll look back and see that you're much more aware of the impact of each of your choices, while having moved personally to a place of greater prosperity, security, and appreciation of life.

PART I

GREEN YOUR LIFE

CHAPTER 1

BUSTiNG GREEN MYTHS

Over the years, I've heard many individuals complain that going green is too expensive or that recycling doesn't help. And I've heard many other green myths that just aren't true. So, here are ten green myths debunked to clear up any misconceptions you may have about all this *green stuff* right up front.

Myth #1: Going Green Will Be Expensive

Busted. This is true for some things but totally false for others. Eating

Green Bite

Americans throw away 2.5 million plastic bottles every hour.[1]

better with organic produce might cost more. Using green alternatives, such as coconut oil for shaving cream, usually costs less than store-bought products. Other green steps might require more cash up front, but they'll save you money for years to come. Installing a water filter at home and using a refillable water bottle can save you thousands of dollars over buying bottled water.

Myth #2: I'll Never Be "Real" Green Because I Can't Afford a Hybrid Car

Busted. With a few small lifestyle changes, you can make more of an eco-wallop than buying a hybrid car ever could. For example, cutting back on how many steaks and burgers you eat can save more energy, water, and greenhouse-gas emissions than driving a hybrid.

Green Bite

With the energy needed to produce a single hamburger, you could drive a small car 20 miles and save about 1,500 gallons of water.[2] Also, just by switching to locally grown produce—instead of buying food that has been trucked or shipped from thousands of miles away—you can cut your carbon footprint way down. (A *carbon footprint* refers to the measure of the impact humans have on the environment in terms of greenhouse gases produced.[3])

Myth #3: We Need More Power Plants

Busted. According to the Natural Resources Defense Council, if we become more energy efficient, we'll have all the energy we need. Switching over lighting in the U.S. to more energy-efficient compact-fluorescent or LED lighting would save billions of dollars and cut the need for 24 power plants. Hundreds of other sectors could see improvements like this as well. It's similar to telling a very obese person that they can thrive on half the calories they consume. Once we get in shape and efficient, we can meet all our needs easier.

Myth #4: I've Heard That Compact Fluorescent Lights Contain Mercury, and That's a Big Problem

Busted. Yes, today's compact fluorescent lightbulbs (CFLs) do contain a speck of mercury—about four milligrams each, which is less than the amount in a watch battery. But heck, an old-fashioned

Green Bite

A power plant will emit 10 milligrams of mercury to produce the electricity needed to power an incandescent bulb over the course of its lifetime, but only 2.4 milligrams to power a CFL for the same amount of time—saving about 7.6 milligrams of mercury from going up in smoke.[4]

And, many communities are set up to recycle CFLs to make certain that the mercury is used over and over again.

mercury thermometer has about 500 milligrams of mercury, and older home thermostats had up to 3,000 milligrams.[4]

And here's the good news for your naysayer friends: Compact fluorescents actually save you from mercury poisoning. Coal- and gas-burning power plants spew mercury in the air when they make electricity. CFLs use two-thirds less electricity than Edison's incandescent lamps, so less mercury ends up in the atmosphere.

Myth #5: Solar Panels Are Way Too Expensive— I'll Never Be Able to Afford Them

Busted. Solar-electric panels are actually the last thing you want to install in your home or office if you're going green. Say what? It's true! You can save more energy for a lot less cash by going energy efficient first—*before* taking the plunge for solar panels. For every dollar you spend to conserve energy, you can save $5 to $100 (or more) on the cost of a solar-electric system. Here's the math: Replacing just ten standard incandescent bulbs with energy-efficient lighting, which uses only a third of the energy, will cost between $20 and $50. And you'd save about $20 each month in electricity. A solar-electric system that would generate that same $20 of electricity each month would cost about $4,000.

Myth #6: Sure, Changing Lights Might Be a Good Investment, but Other Items Will Take Too Many Years to Pay Back—I Won't Be Around That Long

Busted. Every green investment, from using recycled batteries to installing a new Energy Star air-conditioning unit, will have a different rate of return financially and for the energy and resources saved. But many financial paybacks take only one to three years.

Green Bite

Adobe Systems, Inc., spent $1.4 million retro-fitting three buildings with new energy- and water-saving technologies. In the first year, the company saved more than $1 million on energy and water costs. And the market value of those buildings increased by $10 million.[5] Those same types of returns are available to everyone.

Myth #7: Small Changes Don't Matter

Busted. Millions of people making small changes create a huge impact.

Green Bite

"If everyone in the country elected to buy one package of 100 percent recycled napkins instead of the non-recycled variety, that act alone would save one million trees."

— **Jennifer Powers**, spokeswoman for the Natural Resources Defense Council

Myth #8: Keeping Older Appliances Is Better Than Buying New Ones

Busted. Changing to energy-efficient appliances will dramatically lower your energy bills. There is some truth to this myth, however. New models do contain a hefty amount of *embodied energy,* which is the amount of energy used to mine and refine metals or even recycle old products and turn them into new appliances. Then to package appliances and ship or truck them to their new homes also requires a great deal of energy.

Green Bite

Many new appliances, especially refrigerators, can save 50 to 70 percent on energy over 1970s or 1980s models. It takes only a couple years for the energy savings to pay for the energy to build a new appliance—known as Energy Returned on Energy Invested (EROEI)—especially if you take advantage of rebates being offered. The Website **www.energystar .gov** has a full listing of rebates.

Myth #9: It's Better to Leave Computers On; Turning Them On and Off Wears Them Out Faster

Busted. In the past, it was true that older computers didn't like to be turned on and off very often, but all that has changed. You can save energy, money, and all the associated environmental impacts by turning your computer and monitor off when you're not using them.

> **Green Bite**
>
> Pick up a Smart Power or WattStopper power strip that will automatically shut off all your peripherals (such as printers) when it senses you've turned off your computer. This will prevent power vampires—invisible "leaks" of electricity that some appliances use, even when they appear to be off. See **www. NewLeafAmerica.com**.

Myth #10: There's Nothing Wrong with Buying Plastic—It's All Recycled Today

Busted. No, unfortunately, it's not. Only #1 and #2 plastics get a new life as playground equipment or ski parkas. Vinyl or PVC (polyvinyl chloride) can leach heavy metals into landfills and spread nasties like dioxin into the air.

> **Green Bite**
>
> Adopt the mantra: *No #3 or V, please.*
>
> The symbols *#3* and *V* stand for PVC or vinyl. If you have old shower curtains, boots, or raincoats, get them to a hazardous-waste site for disposal rather than tossing them in the garbage (where they'll end up in a landfill).

CHAPTER 2

GREEN YOUR WARDROBE

I wrote a poem the first week I was traveling in India several years ago about being seduced by an incredible woman. I was in love with her voice, the way she smelled, but mostly her visual beauty. The woman was India herself—this land so rich with colors and textures was, without a doubt, a feminine country. No stereotypical male energy of rules or organization or practicality had broken this goddess.

It's no wonder that the British couldn't continue ruling there and eventually left. With the spark of the divine feminine, she was too wild to be tamed into the linear order so prevalent in industrialized countries. She was a whirl of temple bells in the early morning, the aroma of curry and rice so thick my eyes would water when I walked past the street booths, and colors more alive than any I'd ever laid eyes on.

The silk saris of the women of India were a match for even a field of the Creator's most vibrant flowers. I'd heard that the wealthiest class of women may wear a sari only a couple of times and would then hand it down to a staff person or employee, who after a while would hand it down to someone else, and on and on down the community silk route it would flow. Eventually, maybe years later, those golden threads would make their way to the lowliest of families—the ones living off the land, usually by a stream or river.

A few huts would be clustered together, each one no bigger than a bedroom in the States. There were no washing machines or dryers, and no electricity to power them anyway. The women washed clothes by the edge of the river. Over and over again they'd slap the wet fabric on a rock, an unchoreographed dance of random whirls of colors arching through the air. Afterward, they'd stretch their wet saris out on flat rocks to bake dry in the afternoon sun. Before sunset, the women would return and neatly fold their prized, and sometimes only, possessions.

And each morning, these women would pull back the burlap drape that kept the flies and sun out of the interior of their mud huts and emerge into a new day looking like they'd just stepped off a fashion-show runway. Their dresses spotless, neatly pressed by the sun, and as vibrant as sunlight through stained glass, the women shone with smiles that touched everyone they met.

When a sea of these gems of fabrics filled the market or streets, it was almost too much for the eyes to take. Patterns and colors that Western-ers would never dream of putting together were everywhere. Canary yellow, violet, gold, greens, blues—all mixed in a symphony of color.

I was never able to find that poem once I got back to the States. I guess some things are better off just left to memory.

What we choose to wear and adorn our bodies with is as personal a choice and expression as we have. For some, walking the dark green path of find-ing or buying preloved clothing will be an exciting adventure. Others might cringe at the thought of wearing what was already owned by another. What-ever your path, I've added some food for thought about the impact of your clothing choices.

Make Green Easy

✓Cold Wash and Line Dry

Washing and dry cleaning take the biggest eco-toll on clothing. Buy fabrics that don't require dry cleaning if possible. Try washing in cold water only. The entire country of Japan has been wash-ing clothes in cold water for as far back as anyone can remember. Your clothes and colors will last longer, and you'll save energy and money by not using heated water. Also, try line drying on warm days to go even further down the green road.

✓*Love What's Already in Your Closet*

The greenest clothes are the ones already hanging in your closet. No extra resources are required to manufacture them, no fossil fuels or packaging to ship them, no retail stores needed to sell them . . . and no additional cost to you.

✓*Buy Clothing and Fashions That Last*

That trendy garb might be hip this summer, but will you love it in three or five years? Classic clothing that lasts is always a good bet. If you want to be edgy, look for preloved clothing at second-hand shops, vintage stores, or online.

Keep clothing longer by mending a broken button or tear. That's much more environmentally and fiscally responsible than tossing it and buying something new.

✓*Swap or Trade*

For a unique clothing opportunity, visit the Website **www.swaporamarama.org**, a clothing swap and series of do-it-yourself workshops in which a community explores creative reuse through the recycling of used clothing.

You can trade clothing online with other hip rehashers at **www.rehashclothes.com**.

✓*Recycle—Don't Trash*

Goodwill, The Salvation Army, many churches, and other nonprofits will gladly take your old but still good threads for either resale or turning into rags or other uses.

Patagonia has a Common Threads Garment Recycling Program that recycles fleece garments from any manufacturer and has them melted down and spun into new fabric, saving over 80 percent of the energy and 70 percent of the CO_2 used in making virgin polyester. Patagonia also accepts cotton T-shirts and recycles them to good use. Wash your T-shirts and fleece and mail them off to: Patagonia Service Center, ATTN: Common Threads Recycling Program, 8550 White Fir Street, Reno, NV 89523-8939.

The site **www.dressforsuccess.org** accepts donations of wearable women's business clothing and gives them to low-income women searching for jobs. Their phone number is 212-532-1922.

Green Bite

According to **www.trailspace.com**, recycling cotton saves 20,000 liters of water per kilogram of cotton, plus pesticides, fuel, and fertilizer.

✔ *Make Old T-shirts New Again*

Everyone has a favorite old T-shirt from some event, concert, or memory that they don't wear but can't part with. It can be easily turned into a pillow (stuffed with other recycled clothing), or even a lady's halter top with a little creative cutting and sewing.

✓ *Try Vintage or Preloved*

Want to make the best eco-choice if you need something new? Hunt for bargains and one of a kinds at thrift stores or vintage-clothes shops. Very little new energy and no virgin fabric is used in preloved clothing. There are even boutiques that sell or consign high-end designer labels.

✓ *Know Your Green Fabrics*

— *Organic cotton.* Fabric choices can be radically different in their eco-impact. Conventionally grown cotton accounts for a quarter of all the pesticides used in the United States. When you need new undergarments or clothing, go for organic. You know you won't have any residual poisons in your drawers, and you'll be helping to support a sustainable farmer.

— *Hemp.* Hemp cloth is more durable than cotton and far superior to any other plant fabric environmentally. It's one of the fastest-growing biomasses on the planet, producing 250 percent more fiber than cotton and 600 percent more fiber than flax grown on the same land; and it requires little to no pesticides or fertilizers.

The U.S. is presently the only industrialized country where hemp is illegal to grow, although individual states are passing pro-hemp laws to override the outdated federal restrictions, which link hemp to its distant cousin *Cannabis sativa* (marijuana). Buying hemp-fabric clothing strengthens this important industry, which can play a huge role in our planetary shift to sustainability.

— *Plant-based synthetics.* An alternative to fossil-fuel-based synthetic fabrics are those made from polymers derived from plants. Ingeo is one that's made from corn by-products fermented and transformed into fibers and fabric. Ingeo offers some of the advantages of other synthetics, such as strength and wicking properties without using petroleum as its base. Versace is one of the designer-clothing firms using Ingeo, under the trade name NatureWorks. REI carries Teko brand hiking socks made from Ingeo.

— *Limit polyester and synthetics.* Polyester and other synthetic fabrics are made from petroleum and require large amounts of energy to convert that substance into fabrics. They're great for some specialty applications like rain gear, but for everyday wear, consider another choice. The process releases volatile organic compounds, particulate smog, and acids such as hydrogen chloride into the atmosphere. All of them can cause or aggravate respiratory disease. The Environmental Protection Agency's (EPA) Resource Conservation and Recovery Act considers many textile-manufacturing facilities, which dump toxins in waterways, to be hazardous-waste generators.

— *Bamboo.* Surprisingly soft and luxurious fabrics can be made from bamboo, one of the world's fastest-growing plants. Clothing made from bamboo also contains natural antibacterial properties. However, most of the bamboo fabric is imported from the Far East and thus carries with it a hefty carbon-footprint tag.

— *Recycled fabrics*. Patagonia also recycles plastic soda bottles. They melt down the plastic and spin it into fibers that are woven into fabrics such as polar fleece.

You can go to **www.whitesierra.com** for sportswear made from bamboo, hemp, linen blends, organic cotton, and recycled "soda-bottle shirts."

Green Bite

Hemp has been the most sustainable and useful plant on the planet for over 10,000 years. Industrial hemp can sustainably replace many eco-destructive practices and products, and can be used in the creation of tree-free paper, fabric, plastics, and even biofuels. The Declaration of Independence was drafted by Thomas Jefferson on hemp paper, yet hemp was outlawed in the U.S. in 1937, the same year that DuPont patented and introduced petroleum-based nylon.

Cultivating hemp locally could provide biofuel, hemp-based building materials, food, oil, and numerous other products without the environmental damage from petroleum-based alternatives. Studies by the Dutch government in 1993 confirmed what the U.S. Department of Agriculture discovered 80 years ago: an acre of hemp produces four times as much paper as an acre of trees. Researchers at the Wood Materials and Engineering Laboratory at Washington State University have used the plant to develop medium-density fiberboard that's stronger than wood.

Resources

Here are some sites to start your search for green clothing and shoes:

- **www.planetearthstreetwear.com**: A green-label brand that uses sustainable fabrics.

- **www.lilikoiclothing.com**: Features women's eco-friendly, hip, and attractive clothing made ethically with sustainable fabrics.

- **www.kava.com**: Offers a line of bamboo, soy, and hemp shirts, pullovers, and pants.

- **www.golite.com**: Sells backpacking shirts made from coconut shells that were discarded by restaurants and food manufacturers.

- **www.nosweatapparel.com**: Fair-trade and union-made clothing; some organic, and some from Bethlehem in the hopes of promoting peace in the Middle East.

- **www.timberland.com**: Provides the equivalent of nutritional labels for its shoes that tell what's inside, from recycled rubber to the energy used in production.

- **www.keenfootwear.com**: Offers sneakers that use recycled-aluminum eyelets, non-synthetic and biodegradable rubber, and natural water-based glues.

- **www.tomsshoes.com**: For every pair of shoes sold, Toms will donate a pair to a needy child. I couldn't find how eco-friendly the shoes are, but this is a cool idea that definitely resonates with the shift in consciousness that's happening.

- **www.soles4souls.com**: Donate your worn but good shoes, and Soles4Souls will distribute them to people in need around the world.

- **www.solesunited.com**: Mail your old Crocs in, and they'll be ground up and remanufactured into new shoes.

- **www.greenpeople.org**: Search for local green stores with a zip-code search engine.

- **www.organicexchange.org**: You can find online retailers and stores that carry organic fabric clothing and apparel.

- **www.patagonia.com**: Durable, quality clothes from organic and recycled fabrics; lifetime warranty.

CHAPTER 3

GREEN YOUR

PERSONAL-CARE

PRODUCTS

When crude oil first was discovered in Pennsylvania in 1859, Robert Chesebrough was a young chemist working on distilling fuel from whale oil. His work was rendered obsolete when the whale-oil market crashed after the unearthing of crude. So he headed to Titusville, Pennsylvania, to see if the newly discovered "black gold" had any commercial potential. When he got there, he found a waste product called "rod wax," a goo that stuck to the drill bit and caused the drilling rigs to seize up if it wasn't removed. Rod wax was thrown aside except on the occasion when a driller would slap some of the thick sticky stuff on a cut or scrape to stop the bleeding.

Chesebrough took the black rod wax back to his laboratory to see if it had any value. He discovered that by distilling it down, he could create a lighter-colored wax. In 1872, Mr. Chesebrough patented the process of making petroleum jelly. His petroleum jelly is still popular today. Moms use it on children for rashes and burns.

Petrolatum, another name for petroleum jelly, is listed as a probable human carcinogen in the European Union's Dangerous Substances Directive (UNECE 2004). Its use in cosmetics was banned in the EU in 2004, with the following caveat: ". . . if the full refining history is known and it can be shown that the substance from which it is produced is not a carcinogen."[1]

Wait, we've been using petroleum jelly for decades—it has to be safe. Think again! Petroleum jelly is considered a cosmetic, and the FDA doesn't approve or reject cosmetics. Cosmetic manufacturers are not required to have preapproval, safety testing, or provide proof of performance claims before offering products to consumers. The 1938 Food, Drug, and Cosmetic Act requires manufacturers only to list the ingredients and provide warning labels. Soaps and shampoos that make any "body enhancing" claims such as deodorizing or moisturizing are considered cosmetics and need only to list their ingredients.[1]

"True" soaps, in which the bulk of ingredients are an alkali and fatty acids, are regulated by the Consumer Product Safety Commission, not the FDA, and do not require ingredient labeling. The nonprofit Environmental Working Group (EWG) found the carcinogen known as 1,4-dioxane in 28 percent of all personal-care products after an exhaustive study of ingredients in over 27,000 products.[1] Of all products assessed, 80 percent contained ingredients that can be contaminated with impurities linked to cancer and other health problems, including more than 80 percent of all lip balms and bath products for babies.[2]

The good news is that because of the work of consumer protection groups like Skin Deep, manufacturers using toxic products are being outed and pressured to change. More than 500 manufacturers have signed on to the voluntary Compact for Safe Cosmetics, which aims to remove toxins from cosmetics and personal-care products. (Many mega companies have yet to sign on.) The European Union prohibits the use of known or suspected carcinogens, mutagens, and reproductive toxins (also known as CMRs) from cosmetics. And California has enacted its own legislation banning carcinogens or reproductive-organ disrupters in cosmetics.[1]

It can be overwhelming to realize that many of the products you put on your body have been manufactured with the goal of sales and profit foremost—not your personal health, not the well-being of animals, and not the impact that these products have on various ecosystems. This isn't surprising. It's simply a result of how the old paradigm of corporate structures was established: profit before people. It's time for a change and a new direction—*doing well by doing good*. And a great place to start the green transition is with those items you use every day.

Make Green Easy

✓*Getting Started*

Gather up all of the personal-care products you presently use and read the labels. If they contain any of the toxins listed at the end of this chapter, ask yourself if you want to continue using those products and supporting the companies that make them. Purchase a few all-purpose organic products (Dr. Bronner's Magic Soap is a great one to start with), and go forward on your path from there. Keep it simple, and enjoy the journey toward a healthier life and planet.

✓*Check Products on "Skin Deep"*

The Skin Deep Website (**www.cosmeticsdata base.com**) offers side-by-side comparisons of more than 25,000 products. Like cosmetics, the list of toxins in personal-care products is overwhelming. With a little research and some label reading, you can find safe, nontoxic shampoos, conditioners, and other products or alternatives that are safer for you, your family, and the planet.

✓*Beware of Complimentary Toiletries*

When you're traveling, remember to bring your own safe soaps and shampoos with you. Those cute but highly packaged convenience bottles at your hotel may not be the best items to bring back into your home. Check the labels, and if there isn't a list of ingredients, beware. If they're not healthy products for humans or the planet, write a nice note to the manager suggesting alternatives.

There's a growing number of "green hotels" that are providing customers with better choices in food, personal care, indoor air quality, and amenities. The Website **www.greenhotels.com** lists numerous hotels that "are committed to encouraging, promoting, and supporting ecological consciousness in the hospitality industry."

✓ *Bath Salts*

Many bath salts contain borax and synthetic fragrances that cause reactions in some people. Borax is unavailable in parts of Europe because of concerns with birth defects and problems with the reproductive organs of children after exposure. It's recommended that pregnant women and children are better off not having exposure to Borax[2]. For an alternative, try straight Epsom salt, Dead Sea salt, or the following recipe:

Better bath salts: Mix 3 cups Epsom salt, 1 cup baking soda, and ½ cup table salt in a bowl. Add fresh rosemary, lavender, or natural oils of your choosing. Enjoy.

✓ *Bubble Bath*

Soaking in a bath can be a healthy and calming experience. The challenge is that most commercial bubble baths contain toxins, synthetic fragrances, and often DEA (or diethanolamine, a product that over time can reformulate with other ingredients to create carcinogens[3]). In addition, children are much more sensitive to these chemicals than adults. The FDA has received complaints of skin rashes and urinary tract, bladder, and kidney infections from people taking bubble baths.[4] Aubrey Organics (**www.aubrey-organics.com**) carries a line of safe bubble baths.

Homemade bubble bath: You'll need: 1 pint distilled warm water, half of a 4-ounce bar of castile soap, 2 ounces liquid glycerin, and essential oils such as lavender or orange oil. In a bowl, shave the soap into the warm water and add glycerin. Mix, and let sit. Once the ingredients have softened, blend until smooth with a wooden spoon; add essential oils, if desired, to the mixture. Store in a mason jar.

✓*Shampoos*

Many shampoos contain DEA, which can turn into a carcinogen. In fact, this chemical has been banned in Europe. (See the Green Bite at the end of this chapter for more info on DEA.) Carefully examine labels, and check out these better options:

- Pure Essentials Fragrance-Free Shampoo
- Giovanni's Tea Tree Triple Treat Shampoo
- Granny's Old-Fashioned Shampoo
- Dr. Bronner's soaps
- Aubrey Organics shampoos

✓*Conditioners*

Most mainstream and many "natural" conditioners have been found to contain trace carcinogens or compounds such as benzalkonium chloride, which can be irritating to the eyes and skin.

Mayonnaise or yogurt conditioner: Massage mayonnaise or plain yogurt into hair and scalp. Leave it on for 15 minutes. Rinse well with warm water.

Coconut-oil conditioner: My wife, Becky, massages a bit of organic coconut oil in her hair and sometimes leaves it in all day. It's a great conditioner, especially after her chlorine-saturated swim in the local pool.

✓ Soaps

Pure castile soaps and glycerin soaps with natural oils are much better than soaps listing 45 ingredients that you can't pronounce. Some good commercial brands are Dr. Bronner's and Sirena Pure Coconut Oil Soap.

✓ Body and Baby Powders

Conventional body powders contain talc, a ground-up stone, which can be a carcinogen when inhaled. The FDA reported that in their tests of 40 brands of talc, 39 contained asbestos.[4] Powders may also contain synthetic chemical fragrances and dyes to which many people have reactions.

Cornstarch powder or potato flour: Natural cornstarch and potato flour work wonderfully as a baby or grown-up powder. Add natural spices right before using if you want a scent.

✓Massage Oils

Conventional body oils may contain chemical fragrance, dyes, and preservatives, which are often based on mineral oil, a petroleum derivative that can clog pores.

Natural massage oil: Use natural organic oils, such as coconut, avocado, jojoba, and olive oils, as well as various nut oils. Refrigerate your natural massage oil to prevent it from going rancid.

✓Deodorants and Antiperspirants

Deodorants and antiperspirants both fight odor. Deodorants inhibit the growth of bacteria, which cause odor; and antiperspirants stop perspiration by blocking the skin's pores. The FDA warns against using deodorant soaps on infants under six months old.[4] Check the label.

The aluminum in most conventional antiperspirants is a strong neurotoxicant (toxic to the nervous system). Aluminum may also be linked to the onset of Alzheimer's disease, but the evidence isn't conclusive. You may want to avoid products containing aluminum.

As an alternative, try using natural deodorants that use crystals from mineral salts and that don't contain aluminum. Check out **www.basin.com** for aluminum-free deodorants.

✓Chemical Hair Removers

Be very careful. Chemical hair removers work by breaking down the hair's keratin. The challenge is that skin also contains keratin, and some people experience burning or allergic reactions when these products come into contact with their skin. Rinse well if you do use them.

✓ Facial Cleansers

Here are some safer soaps for tender faces:

- Sirena Pure Coconut Oil Soap
- Kiss My Face Pure Olive Oil Soap
- Dr. Bronner's Baby Supermild Soap
- Dr. Bronner's Unscented Baby
  Castile Liquid Soap

Oatmeal cleanser: To make this natural facial cleanser, chop rolled oats in a food processor or blender until fine. Massage a small amount into wet skin. Rinse.

✓ Facial Masks

Many of these products contain numerous toxic ingredients, including synthetic fragrances and carcinogenic dyes. Here are a couple alternatives you can make:

Oatmeal and honey mask: Mix together a ½ cup of oatmeal and 2 tablespoons of honey. Apply to face, and leave on for at least 30 minutes.

Meringue mask: Combine 2 egg whites and 1 vitamin E capsule, and whip until stiff. Spread the mask on your face, allow it to dry, and then rinse.

green your personal-care products

✓ Shaving Creams

Many conventional shaving creams are full of synthetic chemicals that are potentially carcinogenic, hormone disrupting, and irritating.[3]

Green shaving cream: Try using 100 percent aloe vera for a slick, natural shaving gel. You can buy aloe-vera gel, or use fresh aloe right from the plant. Just cut open a leaf and rub onto your skin. Coconut butter or oil also works well as a natural shaving cream.

✓ Styling Mousses and Gels

Again, it's important to read the labels. Many styling products contain toxic ingredients, including DEA.

Gelatin mousse: Mix together 2 cups of boiling water, 1 teaspoon of powdered gelatin, and 1 teaspoon of vinegar. Strain through a coffee filter into a sprayer bottle.

✓ Sunscreens

Look at the sunscreen you may have at home. You'll probably find a warning label that says something like this: "Keep out of reach of children. Use on infants under six months, only with the advice of a physician." If the chemicals in your sunscreen aren't healthy for infants, how can they be healthy for adults or the plants and animals in the oceans, lakes, and rivers that these chemicals get washed into? One brand I found even stated, "Flammable. Do not use near flame." Look, Mom—it's a sunscreen and fire starter all in one!

An Australian campaign to lower skin-cancer risk recommends protective clothing and shading first, with sunscreen only as a last resort. Here are some better choices for sunscreen:

- Aubrey Organics Ultra 15 Natural Herbal Sunblock
- Kiss My Face Sun Screen
- Dr. Levine's Ultimate Sun Block
- Badger Sunscreen
- UV Natural Sunscreen

✓ *Toothpaste*

Have you ever read the warning label on many commercially available toothpastes? "Do not swallow. If you swallow more than the amount normally used for brushing, seek professional help or contact a poison control center immediately." Come on, manufacturers! Please make products that are safe and healthy to put into and on our bodies.

Green Bite

Say no to DEA! DEA is widely used in personal-care products because it builds a thick lather in shampoos and helps thicken lotions and creams. By itself, it isn't harmful, but in storage in a warehouse, on a store shelf, or in a cabinet at home, this chemical can re-act with other ingredients in the product and form a toxic carcinogen. The danger is that DEA cannot be easily purged from the body, and it builds up over time.[5]

Better toothpastes: Look for brands that contain simple, healthy ingredients (without warning labels). These include Tom's of Maine, Natural Dentist Healthy Teeth & Gums Toothpaste, and Jason Healthy Mouth Tea Tree Toothpaste.

✓*Avoid These Ingredients*

- Cocamide DEA
  (or Cocamide Diethanolamine)

- DEA Lauryl Sulfate
  (or Diethanolamine Lauryl Sulfate)

- Lauramide DEA
  (or Lauramide Diethanolamine)

- Linoleamide DEA
  (or Linoleamide Diethanolamine)

- Oleamide DEA
  (or Oleamide Diethanolamine)

- Any product containing TEA or Triethanolamine

CHAPTER 4
GREEN YOUR COSMETICS

Throughout history, makeup trends have come and gone. Whatever your feelings are about cosmetics, they have been a part of human culture for at least 5,000 years. In ancient Egypt, men and women decorated their eyelids with dark green clay and used soot for mascara. During the European Middle Ages, when pale skin was a sign of wealth, people would apply a toxic white-lead paint, which also contained arsenic, to their faces. Some even went to the extreme of "bleeding" to look authentically pale. During the 1800s, society women would use belladonna eyedrops to dilate their eyes and raise their heartbeat. At the time, the dreamy, dilated stare produced from the poisonous reaction was thought to be most attractive. However, prolonged use caused blindness. Belladonna or deadly nightshade is the most toxic plant found in the Northern Hemisphere, and consuming just one leaf could be fatal. Oh, the price of vanity!

One would think that, after a few thousand years, we'd learn not to use poisons on our skin. We know that skin absorbs chemicals. For instance, applying nicotine or morphine patches to the skin has been proven to be a very effective way to administer these drugs. Many of us assume that cosmetics have been tested for safety—but sadly, most aren't.

The official statement from the U.S. Food and Drug Administration Website is as follows: "The regulatory requirements governing the sale of cosmetics are not as stringent as those that apply to other FDA-regulated products. . . . Manufacturers may use any ingredient or raw material, except for color additives and a few prohibited substances, to market a product without a government review or approval."

In 2005, the Campaign for Safe Cosmetics found that only 11 percent of the 10,500 ingredients used in cosmetics are ever tested for safety or toxicity. In addition, fragrances are considered to have trade secrets, so manufacturers don't have to disclose their ingredients at all.

It turns out that some lipsticks still contain lead. A chemical linked to birth defects is a common ingredient in nail polish. Sunscreens and mascara may contain the same carcinogen used in cleaners and floor polish. Fragrances are known to cause allergies and trigger asthma. In low levels, these may not pose high risks; however, we're often exposed to industrial chemicals from many different sources on a daily basis, including cleaners, personal-care products, and cosmetics. It all adds up.

Fortunately, there's good news in store for those who don't want to give up their cosmetics entirely. Many companies are genuinely concerned with their products' impact on our health and the environment. Healthy alternatives are becoming more available, and people are demanding better regulation.

The organization Teens for Safe Cosmetics is holding national campaigns to bring awareness into schools. In 2004, the European Union passed an amendment to their Cosmetics Directive that prohibits the use of known or suspected carcinogens, mutagens, and reproductive toxins (CMRs) in cosmetics. By January 2008, more than 500 product manufacturers had voluntarily signed the Compact for Safe Cosmetics.

The companies listed on the Website **www .safecosmetics.org** have pledged to "not use chemicals that are known or strongly suspected of causing cancer, mutation or birth defects in their products and to implement substitution plans that replace hazardous materials with safer alternatives in every market they serve." Unfortunately, the largest and most well-known cosmetics manufacturers haven't signed on yet.

California Takes the Lead

California passed the California Safe Cosmetics Act of 2005, and it went into effect in 2007. The act requires cosmetic companies to notify state health authorities if a product contains any ingredient— including "trade secrets" and "proprietary," ingredients—listed on California's Proposition 65. (This is a group of chemicals deemed carcinogenic by the International Agency for Research on Cancer, the EPA, the National Toxicology Program [NTP], the FDA, or the National Institute for Occupational Safety and Health.) In addition, companies must report the ingredients considered reproductive toxins by the NTP's Center for the Evaluation of Risks to Human Reproduction.

Make Green Easy

✓ *Keep It Simple*

Simplify your routine. Use fewer products, and include only those that you know are safe. This is one more way to support only the companies that are doing good for people and the planet. As I mentioned, examine the ingredients in the items you already use, and consult Skin Deep's Website (**www.cosmeticsdatabase.com**), which offers comparisons of thousands of products. The list of toxic chemicals in cosmetics is already too long for anyone to attempt to recall while shopping, and many ingredients have multiple names. With a little research and some label reading beforehand, you can find safe nontoxic cosmetics that would even make Cleopatra envious.

✓ *Go Fragrance Free*

Synthetic scents are often derived from petro-chemicals and may cause skin irritation and other problems. Essential oils are a way to have a hint of nature like lavender or lilac, without any toxic risk.

✓ *Look for the Humane Cosmetics Standard Label*

Testing cosmetics on animals is unnecessary and unethical. Safe products won't bother animals or humans. Look for the Humane Cosmetics Standard (HCS) label. Animal-welfare groups estimate that 38,000 animals die needlessly in the European Union every year in tests for new products. Essential oils are a way to have a hint of nature like lavendar or lilac, without any toxic risk.

✓ *Know What Organic, Natural, Pure, and Gentle Mean on Labels*

Be wary of these marketing words, which have no certification or guidelines. Read the ingredients on the label. There is no legal definition of what is or isn't "natural." And just because something comes from a plant or is "all natural," it doesn't mean that it's safe. Remember belladonna? Even Botox is derived from natural botulism bacteria, one of the strongest toxins known. Products claiming to be organic are not, unless they've been certified "USDA Organic." Again, check the Skin Deep Website to make sure that the products you're using don't contain toxins or other harmful ingredients.

✓ Buy Certified-Natural Products

The European Union enacted the German BDIH certification, which requires ingredients to be petroleum, synthetic, and preservative free, with no animal testing. BDIH certification also requires independent testing and encourages the use of certified-organic or wild-harvested botanical ingredients whenever possible. Several U.S. manufacturers have received this prestigious certification for their products, including the following companies:

- www.AlimaPure.com
- www.USA.Weleda.com

✓ Find Out More Before Botox

Injecting botulinum toxin in the forehead may help one's looks, but it can be dangerous and carries possible side effects. For instance, the botulinum toxin can spread beyond the injection site. In addition, the FDA is currently reviewing the safety of the drug after receiving "reports of systemic adverse reactions including respiratory compromise and death." Death—that's pretty severe. (Approximately one microgram of botulism is lethal to humans.) One study found that 23 percent of people who received Botox injections would have been better off spending their money on therapy because they suffered from low self-worth and body-image issues.

✓ Hair Dyes

Your scalp absorbs trace amounts of the chemicals in hair dye. This is especially significant (and potentially dangerous) during pregnancy. Dark colors often contain possibly harmful coal-tar derivatives. In addition, ethanolamine, potassium persulfate, and sodium persulfate are common ingredients and need careful handling and rinsing.

Safe hair-dye alternatives: Henna and plant materials will color your hair much more gently and without the toxins or ammonia. Some dark-haired beauties swear by a coffee rinse as a gentle way to ease any gray.

✓ Hair Spray

Reading the warnings on a bottle of hair spray should be enough to raise concern: "Avoid spraying near eyes. Keep out of reach of children. Use only as directed. Flammable." Common ingredients include carcinogenic PVP (polyvinylpyrrolidone) and formaldehyde. In addition, hair-spray users risk developing thesaurosis (an abnormal retention of foreign substances). Enough said!

Rosemary-water hair spray: Place a handful of dried rosemary sprigs in a French press or mug with boiling water. Allow to steep and cool for a couple of hours. Strain and place in a spray bottle. Spritz as needed.

✓ *Hair Straighteners*

Many hair straighteners contain human placenta, the nutrient-rich life organ that's expelled when an infant is born. Products made with placenta may contain extra estrogen hormones, which have been linked to early-onset puberty, especially in young African-American girls who are more prone to use these products.

✓ *Lip Gloss*

Lip balm commonly contains phenol, a poisonous chemical also used as a pesticide, which can be absorbed by the skin. Adverse reactions include vomiting, nausea, convulsions, paralysis, and even death. Very small amounts can cause rashes, swelling, pimples, and hives. Lip glosses and balms may also contain plasticizers such as microcrystalline wax and polyisobutane, both of which are allergens.

Healthy alternative lip gloss: Vitamin E gel can be bought in small containers and makes a great lip gloss that moisturizes, protects, and adds a bit of shine.

✓ *Makeup Removers*

Makeup removers may contain a host of nasties, especially petroleum-based carcinogens, which can easily penetrate the skin.

Natural makeup remover: Combine 1 tablespoon each of castor oil, light olive oil, sunflower oil, and safflower oil. (Use organic oils.) Blend ingredients. It's perfect for removing makeup around the eyes.

✓*Moisturizers*

Lotions and moisturizers are basically a mixture of water and oil with an emulsifier added to keep the product from separating, and perhaps a preservative. The emulsifier and preservative can be toxic.

Better moisturizers: Use shea butter or coconut oil. Becky loves organic coconut oil for her skin and hair.

✓*Nail Polish and Polish Removers*

The acetone that's relabeled as nail-polish remover may be worse than the toluene, formaldehyde, and phthalatesin contained in the polish you're trying to take off. Look for water-based, nontoxic nail polishes and removers.

✓*Acrylic Nails*

Covering your natural nails in plastic resin causes them to become thin and brittle. It also usually takes a powerful toxic solvent such as acetonitrile to remove the cover. This chemical can irritate the respiratory system and cause an enlarged thyroid. In addition, a fine acrylic dust is stirred up in salons when the acrylic nails are sanded and shaped. That's not good for anybody.

green your cosmetics

✓ *Skin Lighteners*

Many skin lighteners are banned in Europe because they contain hydroquinone. This animal carcinogen, which is toxic to the brain and immune and reproductive systems, is banned in the EU but is still allowed for sale in the U.S.

✓ *Healthy Cosmetics*

Here is a selection of companies that offer safer, more conscientious cosmetics:

- www.inkylovesnature.com
- www.aubrey-organics.com
- www.blackphoenixalchemylab.com
- www.janeiredale.com
- www.larenim.com
- www.miessenceproducts.com
- www.daisybluenaturals.com

CHAPTER 5

GREEN WHAT YOU EAT

One of the first tasks for our homestead in Laguna Beach was to plant some fruit trees. We had a pretty steep slope to work with, so I made some small half-round retaining walls from salvaged broken-up concrete known as riprap or urbanite. These walls would keep the water and nutrients from running down-hill while giving me a leg up to reach the high limbs of the apple and orange trees. As soon as these walls were done, we had a tree-planting party.

Some of the trees, such as the plum, didn't look like much more than a bare twig. Others had a few branches and some leaves. The kumquat still had a few of its sour orange fruits attached. Along with some good friends, we planted our new babies, sang songs, drank wine, and enjoyed a picnic lunch on a blanket beside our new trees.

It's now ten years later, and Becky and I give away more fruit than we could possibly eat from those five trees. And we've added a dozen more fruit bearers over the years to keep them company. The weeks or months when no fruit was ripe gave us the motivation to find out which fruit was in season and to plant that tree. We now have year-round fresh organic fruit just a few steps from our kitchen door.

Where we had only a small spot between some big trees, we planted dwarf lemon and tangerine trees that only grow to about three or four feet around. For some fruit, that's all we want. Over time we filled in under the trees with blueberry bushes, herbs, and strawberries.

Our forest garden is still a work in progress. Becky wants a papaya tree, and she's also nurtured from seed a now one-foot-tall avocado tree she's named Ted. I'd like some more blueberries. But almost every day we take time to be in the garden and acknowledge how grateful we are—and, of course, to grab a fresh snack while we're at it.

Here are some basic concepts to keep in mind in thinking about how and what you eat.

Make Green Easy

✓ *Paper or Plastic? Neither*

When you're asked "Paper or plastic?" just say, "No thanks, I brought my own." Keep a few reusable cloth or string shopping bags in your car, backpack, or bike bag. Some stores will even pay you a nickel for every bag you save. Don't even spend a second trying to figure out if paper bags (made from trees, a renewable resource) are better than plastic ones (made from fossil fuel). They're both "eco-impactors." Plastic bags create less pollution, but many end up in the ocean where unsuspecting marine life ingest them.

✓ *Frequent Your Nearest Farmers Market*

You can find locally grown, seasonal food that's organic at most farmers markets. Plus, it's a great place to mingle and build community ties. To find your nearest farmers market, visit **www. ams.usda.gov/farmersmarkets.**

✓ *Buy Locally Grown Produce*

Look for locally grown produce at your grocery store and farmers market. Did you know that what you eat can have just as much of an impact on your carbon emissions as the kind of car you drive? Many foods travel 1,500 miles or more before they're purchased and consumed. For every calorie of blueberry flown into California from

Chile, the equivalent of about 70 calories of fossil fuel is burned. The supermarket chain Tesco is considering adding food-miles labeling on its products at their U.S. Fresh & Easy stores (**www .FreshandEasy.com**).

✓*Join a Community Supported Agriculture*

A Community Supported Agriculture (CSA) typically is a membership with an organic farmer where you can pick up—or have it delivered to your home—a basket of fresh seasonal produce once or twice a week. Find a CSA near you at **www.local harvest.org**.

✓*Support Organic Growers*

Here are ten excellent reasons to eat organic food and support organic farms.

1. *Organic tastes better.* Try a blind taste test between organic and conventionally grown fruit, and then decide. I've always found that organic produce actually does taste better, and that's priceless.

2. *You'll enjoy better health.* Organic products keep pesticides, herbicides, fungicides, and antibiotics out of your food and drink. These toxins are not easily purged from the body and can compromise your immune system over time.

3. *Organic food is better for kids.* Residual pesticides and chemical fertilizers aren't good for anyone, especially growing children who are more vulnerable to their adverse effects than adults.

4. *Buying organic preserves heirloom species.* Many organic growers are preserving strains of heirloom plants that have stood the test of time—unlike commercial hybrid plants, which are sterile and require growers to purchase new seeds each year. And hybrid plants are susceptible to complete crop loss because they're identical to each other and lack the diversity found in heirloom varieties.

5. *It's better for the soil.* Organic farmers know the value of rich, fertile soil and work to keep building and nurturing their topsoil. Conventional farms add synthetic nutrients to pump up plant growth instead of relying on the naturally occurring nutrients and microbes present in healthy soil.

6. *Organic farms don't use natural gas.* Some 90 percent of conventional fertilizer is made with natural gas, a finite resource that also releases greenhouse gases in its manufacturing process.[1] Organic farms work with nature and are required to use organic compost and soil amendments.

green what you eat

7. *Organic farms don't pollute water sources.* Organic farms don't use harmful chemicals that may leach into the soil, affecting wells and eventually our drinking water.

8. *Organic food supports birds and other wildlife.* Numerous studies have shown that organic farms are inhabited by far more wildlife than conventional farms. Species from butterflies and spiders to migratory birds thrive in areas that contain no harmful chemicals.[2] Many migratory birds are endangered or threatened because of the loss of wetlands and habitat.

9. *It's better for the bees.* On organic farms, bees are thriving, but conventional farms are experiencing devastating losses from colony collapse disorder, which has left some beekeepers with losses of up to 20 to 50 percent.[3] Honeybees are a critical link in food production, pollinating roughly a third of all foods, including more than 100 commercial crops of fruit, vegetables, nuts, and seeds.

10. *Buying organic produce supports family farms.* Small organic farms may be one of the few options left for sustaining the existence of family farms. The USDA predicts that by the year 2010, 60 percent of farm production in the U.S. will come from just 1 percent of farms—all conventional growers. To find an organic farm near you, go to **www.localharvest.org**.

Green Bite

- Raising livestock is responsible for 18 percent of global greenhouse-gas emissions, more than all of the world's transportation sources combined.[4]

- Animals raised for food in the U.S. consume 90 percent of the soy crop, 80 percent of the corn crop, and 70 percent of the grain grown.[5]

- Growing crops for farm animals requires nearly half of the U.S. water supply.[6]

- The meat industry accounts for 70 percent of the water pollution in the U.S.[7]

- An acre of edible crops can feed 20 times as many people as an acre dedicated to cattle.[8]

- Livestock farms are responsible for over one-third of all methane emitted into the atmosphere. Methane is a greenhouse gas that is 23 times as strong as CO_2.[9]

- Nearly 80 percent of the agricultural land in the U.S. is used to raise animals for food. Not all of this land is usable for raising crops. But, it's still a very large amount.

✔*Go Easy on the Meat*

One of the greenest things you can do is eat less meat and fewer dairy products. Some folks who like to calculate these things claim that going vegetarian has a more positive eco-effect than driving a hybrid car. Meat, poultry, and fish contain necessary proteins, but most Americans' diets have too much protein—almost twice the recommended daily allowance. In times past, meat was considered a special addition to the weekly diet, but now because of intensified farming, more meat is being consumed than ever before. And beef is the most eco-taxing of all.

✔*Eat Lower on the Food Chain*

Eating lower on the food chain means that you eat more fruit and vegetables and less meat. And if you eat fish, go with smaller-sized ones. The bigger the fish, the more little fish it has eaten, and the higher the concentration of mercury and other heavy metals that are built up in it. Shark, swordfish, and king mackerel typically contain the highest mercury levels, while salmon, tilapia, and catfish are on the low end. Find out more about safer seafood by visiting the Marine Stewardship Council's Website: **www.msc.org**.

✔*Pick Fresh over Canned*

Always support farmers markets first, but when you do go to a regular market, shop on the outer aisles. That's where you usually find all of the fresh produce. Canned food is great to have on hand for emergencies, but fresh bulk produce uses far less material and energy.

✓ Eat Seasonally Available Foods

Eating foods as they become seasonally available is a wonderful way to reconnect with nature. Also, many feel that it's healthier to eat high-sugar fruits such as grapes in the summer and starches from root crops such as squash and parsnips in the winter when you need the extra calories.

✓ Compost Leftovers and Scraps

Instead of throwing scraps down the drain or in the trash where they're trucked to a landfill, compost them. (Chapter 12 is devoted to this miracle.)

✓ Lighten Up on Packaging

Shop for bulk produce and bring your own bag to carry it home. Farmers markets are a great place to start. Most plastic wrap, shrink-wrap, and other packaging is made from fossil fuels.

✓ Watch the High Fructose Corn Syrup

Check the label on most packaged foods, and you'll see that everything from breakfast cereal to protein bars uses high fructose corn syrup (HFCS), which has been linked to obesity and type 2 diabetes. HFCS is only metabolized in the liver and converts to fat more readily than any other sugar. Other sugars are metabolized in every cell of the body.[10] Look for products made with unrefined sugar or honey.

✓ Look for Antibiotic-Free Eggs and Meat

The use of antibiotics in livestock to reduce disease and promote growth has been controversial for many years. In the U.S., roughly 24 million pounds of antibiotics—about 70 percent of the total amount of antibiotics used in the U.S.—are added to animal feed every year. If only a few bacteria survive the antibiotics, a new and stronger "superbug" is created in our environment. These superbugs are much more difficult to treat when they affect humans.[11] As early as 1963, British researchers tied the emergence of drug-resistant strains of salmonella in humans to antibiotics fed to cattle. Antibiotics were banned from animal feed in Europe beginning in 1995.

✓ Avoid Genetically Engineered Foods

Typically, 60 to 70 percent of the packaged foods on our grocery shelves contain genetically engineered (GE) ingredients. GE foods have had their DNA altered and contain substances that have never been a part of our human food supply. There are about 40 varieties of GE crops approved for consumption in the U.S., and presently manufacturers are not required to label that a product contains GE crops. No long-term studies have been done on the safety of GE foods for humans, animals, or the planet. Certified-organic products cannot contain GE foods, which is another great reason to go organic.

For more information, check out The Campaign (**www.thecampaign.org**). You can help the grassroots campaign pass legislation that would make it mandatory for companies to label products that contain any genetically engineered foods.

Green Bite

The EU, Japan, China, Australia, New Zealand, and many other countries require the mandatory labeling of foods that contain genetically engineered ingredients. As a result, many food manufacturers in those countries choose to use ingredients that weren't genetically modified.[12]

✓ BYO Chopsticks

Grab a cool pair of your own chopsticks, and tuck them in your jacket or purse when you go out for Asian cuisine. Bringing enough for everyone in your party is even better. After dinner, ask for a glass of hot water to dunk and clean. Some trendy spots will even wash your sticks for you, if you ask. You won't halt climate change by bringing your own sticks—and you probably won't save water—but reducing your use of disposables is an easy green step to take.

Green Bite

In China alone, 25 million full-grown trees each year are whittled down for disposable chopsticks.[13] Some creative types are turning these disposable utensils into baskets or other knicknacks. Even better is to reduce the tree cutting by reusing your own sticks before recycling them into something else.

✓ *Eating Well on the Road*

If you're traveling and want to find a restaurant that offers local, seasonal, or vegetarian fare, here are some references to help you:

- **www.eatwellguide.org**: Lists restaurants and stores with seasonal and organic food in the U.S.

- **www.happycow.net**: Includes a guide to restaurants and health-food stores in major cities worldwide

- **www.ivu.org**: Provides links to vegetarian-restaurant guides and news in the U.S. and abroad

CHAPTER 6

GREEN COFFEE AND TEA

It took a second for my eyes to adjust once I was inside. There was a single bare bulb hanging over the cash register. An older lady and young girl were watching television behind the counter. From the age difference, I guessed they were grandmother and granddaughter. The little one was probably eight years old, barefoot, and wearing an oversized yellow T-shirt for a dress.

I wished I had come out earlier, but the midday Brazilian sun was far too hot for my liking. The shelves were half bare, and on display was an odd assortment of U.S. and local brands.

"Café, por favor," I said. The woman gave a warm smile at my attempt at Portuguese and pointed toward the darkest corner of the one-room *mercado*.

I made my way back to the wooden shelves of colorful bags. *Ah, black gold.* I could smell the aroma even through the plastic and foil—it was the local Brazilian coffee grown on this same lush tropical plateau where I stood. I squeezed a few bags in search of whole beans. No luck. All the coffee was already ground. I was a bit disappointed. Apparently, the locals didn't share my obsession with fresh ground coffee.

The bags were lined up on the shelves from the most basic grade at the bottom to the highest grade at the top. I visualized my suitcase and decided that I could probably carry six to eight bags back home. I went for a couple of each brand. *Did I bring enough local money?* The exchange rate was almost two Brazilian reals to one dollar. *Let's see— each of the red bags is 25 reals, so that's $15 U.S. Wait, that can't be right . . .* I squinted at the price again. It was 2.5 reals. That made each one-pound bag of coffee about $1.25. The more expensive ones were about $2.00. I purchased eight bags of coffee in the hopes that the local farmers who grew it would receive most of the $13 and change I spent.

Green Bite

Second only to oil, coffee is the world's most heavily traded commodity. The U.S. is the world's largest coffee importer, reselling coffee at home for about $35 billion for unbrewed beans, and $120 billion for brewed cups of java. At the same time, the countries of production received less than $6 billion.

Make Green Easy

✓ Support Organic Growers

Organic coffee and tea is best for you, the farmer, and the environment. You won't be ingesting residual pesticides and fertilizers, the farmers who grow organically have a healthier workplace, and the environment benefits from unpolluted land and water sources.

✓ Buy Fair Trade

Certified Fair Trade™ coffee and tea typically remove four middlemen in the sales chain from grower to consumer, according to TransFair USA. This ensures a higher wage for those families who actually do the work of growing, as opposed to the two cents that farmers on conventional plantations typically receive from the average $3 cappuccino sold in the U.S. Supporting fair trade also helps promote environmental stewardship in developing countries that currently do not have environmental-protection legislation. Check **www.fairtradefederation.org** for more about this topic.

✓ Go Local

Buying local coffee and tea from the areas closest to you ensures that the least amount of fossil fuel was burned to transport it from grower to your cup. The Kona coast of Hawaii grows some of the best coffee in the world, and it's much closer to the U.S. mainland than Africa or Colombia.

✓Look for Coffee Made in the Shade

Certified shade-grown or "bird friendly" coffee is grown in the shade under a forest canopy and supports much more biodiversity than full-sun plantations, which clear-cut their large trees to create faster growth and increase yields. (Coffee takes longer to ripen in the shade.) Shade-grown plantations can support migratory-bird populations almost as well as a virgin forest, while maintaining the biodiversity of many other species.[1] The more biodiversity, the stronger, more vibrant and more resilient an ecosystem is.

✓BYO Mug

Choose a reusable mug or insulated to-go cup; and you'll be saving paper cups, plastic sipper tops, and cardboard java jackets. Make sure to use an already existing mug from your cupboard, or pick one up secondhand. Ceramics and stainless steel take lots of energy to manufacture, and you may be surprised to read that the Dutch Ministry of Environment (LCA) reports that manufacturing a new ceramic mug takes the same energy as using 294 paper cups.[2]

✓BYO Container for Bulk Tea and Coffee

Bring your own airtight recycled container with you when you buy bulk beans or tea from a coffee shop or market. Sellers today will usually take the time to weigh your container and then deduct that weight when it's filled. You'll save a

Mylar or plastic bag and the smidgen of fossil fuel used to manufacture them.

✓ Use Reusable Filters, Tea Strainers, and More

Coffee filters and tea bags aren't really necessary. You can make great coffee at your home or workplace with a reusable filter or French press. A good stainless-steel tea strainer can allow you to save money with loose tea and keep a lifetime of tea bags out of the landfill. If you still want to use filters and bags, look for ones that are unbleached and biodegradable. Then compost them when done.

✓ Choose Brown Filters

Sometimes it's not practical or feasible to use a French press. If you need a disposable filter, use natural unbleached ones. Traditional white-paper filters use chlorine or dioxin to bleach them. Even better still is to invest in a reusable gold-lined filter.

Green Bite

Styrofoam loses a little mass with each use, meaning that a bit of the product is transferred to the drinks we consume. The EPA has classified styrene (the chemical name for Styrofoam) as a *possible* human carcinogen. Styrofoam can be recycled; however, typically 25 billion Styrofoam cups a year end up in landfills.[3] Countless others are broken up into little pellets that float in oceans and waterways, where it takes a few hundred years for them to break down.

✓ Speak Up

If your local coffee shop doesn't carry "green" coffee and tea, politely ask if they would consider it. Starbucks will brew a cup of fair-trade coffee in a French press, if you ask for it. If the coffee shop you frequent is still using Styrofoam cups, ask them to switch to recycled paper or other alternatives, such as the newer biobased polymers derived from sugar, corn, and soy.

✓ Turn Your Coffeemaker Off

Coffeemakers run only hot water through a filter filled with grounds. They also waste a lot of electricity keeping the coffee hot until they're turned off. If you brew at home, grab a good thermos or air pot (a thermos container with a pump spout) to store your hot beverage. We use a French press, heating just the amount of water we need in a kettle.

✓ Compost the Grounds and Leaves

Add coffee grounds and tea leaves to your compost pile to make an excellent natural fertilizer while keeping a little more waste out of landfills. If you haven't set up a compost pile yet, just dump the spent grounds and leaves around the base of your plants and trees. Coffee grounds contain nitrogen, phosphorus, potassium, and trace elements, which plants (such as azaleas and rosebushes) soak up eagerly when it's mixed with the soil or used as a light mulch.

✓ *Give Green Coffees and Teas for Gifts*

Don't know what to give family members and friends? The best of the best "green" coffees and teas make wonderful gifts and are great icebreakers for sharing the green message. You can even throw in a cool recycled ceramic mug (less energy to manufacture than stainless steel). But stay away from holiday-themed mugs, which won't be used often.

Green Bite

Tea, the second-most consumed beverage in the world after water, wins the lower carbon-footprint award, as it doesn't have to be roasted like coffee. Roasting is typically done with natural gas or electricity, which emits substantial amounts of CO_2. For those who want to really decrease their carbon footprint, locally grown tea uses far less fossil fuel to farm and transport than imported coffee or tea.

You can grow numerous varieties of mint (even chocolate mint), lemongrass, spearmint, peppermint, rose hip, and hibiscus in a container. Even *Camellia sinensis*, the "true tea plant," can be grown in mild climates or brought indoors in winter.

If you'd like to experience a solar cup of joe, check out **www.solarroast.com**. This Colorado-based company uses solar electricity to power its equipment and a focused solar collector to heat up their roasters to 550 degrees Fahrenheit for carbon-zero coffee roasting.

green coffee and tea

CHAPTER 7
GREEN YOUR KIDS

The Great Law of the Iroquois states: "In every deliberation we must consider the impact on the seventh generation . . . even if it requires having skin as thick as the bark of a pine." This long-term perspective of a prominent Native American nation about the impact of our choices on future generations should continue to influence each and every choice we make today. One of the most often-cited definitions of *sustainability* was formed under the leadership of the former prime minister of Norway, Gro Harlem Brundtland, who defines it as: "meeting the needs of the present without compromising the ability of future generations to meet their own needs."

Both the Great Law of the Iroquois and this definition of sustainability emphasize the need that when we're making choices, we must also consider the right of future generations to have healthy, thriving ecosystems and abundant raw materials. Our present system of harvesting nature and then manufacturing, packaging, and distributing goods typically hasn't looked beyond current corporate profit-and-loss statements. And until recently, this process rarely if ever has considered corporate impact on future generations. Fortunately, this is all changing, and the awareness of the legacy and world that we're leaving our children and grandchildren is awakening people to the need for a conscious shift in priorities.

Some may question the economic viability of a completely refocused industrial revolution, in which nature and people matter. Others want to believe it *is* possible, but they may lose faith when friends or family members laugh at the thought of it all. The Great Law of the Iroquois shares its ancient wisdom to guide us through the sea of uncertainty: ". . . even if it requires having skin as thick as the bark of a pine."

Children aren't just miniature adults. Their developing bodies are more vulnerable than an adult's body, and even small doses of unsafe chemicals found in everyday items can adversely affect a child. According to a national survey conducted in the summer of 2007 by the Environmental Working Group: "Every day children are exposed to an average of 27 personal care product ingredients that have not been found safe for kids. . . . Overall, 77 percent of the ingredients in 1,700 children's products reviewed have not been assessed for safety."

Many parents of young children are realizing that, as a whole, their offspring are wiser, more enlightened, and deeper spiritually than past generations. This isn't the first time that a generation has appeared more evolved consciously than their parents. Think about it. Nearly every generation improves on the knowledge base of the past, but no previous ones have focused enough inner work on their own evolving consciousness to realize to such a high degree the nature of that evolution, and then to speak about it and write books describing it.

We must do whatever it takes to guarantee that the incredible children and youth growing up in our world have the resources they need to thrive and carry on the responsibility as stewards of Earth. This isn't an easy task, but as more and more wake up to the importance and urgency of the call to consider the impact on the seventh generation, the transformation will take place.

Make Green Easy

✓ Foster Creativity

Studies have found that creative people excel in both school and life in general. Fostering exploration and play with art, music, and movement will nurture a child's creative seeds for life. Besides the obvious of spending less time glued to the TV, there are other ways to get started.

Playhouses are great. Manufactured playhouses in plastic primary colors hold up well, but they don't inspire much creativity. As an option, use a huge cardboard box from a refrigerator or appliance, and let your kids decorate it themselves with items from nature (including leaves, branches, flowers, and so on) along with paints, crayons, magazine cutouts, or whatever else they like.

Sure, it won't last past summer, but then you'll get to do another project after the playhouse has been turned on its side to become a people crawler or whatever else your child's imagination can dream up. Play silks (as well as other fabrics) provide wonderful tools for creating forts, and they can be reused over and over, taking on unlimited forms and shapes.

A couple of other ideas are to put on a play or just have fun playing dress up (again, inexpensive silks and fabrics provide a wonderful alternative to traditional prepackaged costumes). Turn a scarf into a pirate hat, a belt, a veil . . . the possibilities are endless.

✓ Spend Time in Nature

Instead of the clown, ponies, plastic party hats, or more "stuff," try a birthday celebration in nature at a park, lake, or beach. This alternative can offer inspiration in the form of a nature walk, overnight camping, or a visit to a bird or wildlife sanctuary.

✓ Go for Seconds

If you do want to purchase a manufactured toy, think about buying a slightly worn one. You can find great toys at garage sales; churches; online on craigslist, eBay, and Freecycle; as well as in your local classified ads. When kids outgrow a toy or it's time to let go of one, make sure it finds another good home, or sell it again right where you found it.

✓ Choose Battery Free or Rechargeables

The majority of toys requires batteries, which are not only costly for us to continually buy, but we pay an environmental price from all the batteries that need to be disposed of.

Consider choosing toys that don't require batteries, and for those electronics that do need them, go with high-quality rechargeable ones and a charger. It only takes a couple of times of recharging for the batteries to pay for themselves, and they'll last for hundreds if not thousands of cycles.

Make sure to select batteries that have the same or better ampere-hour rating (amp hr) as the disposables you're used to, and you (and your kids) will be quite content. You can find and read about rechargeable batteries at **www.realgoods.com**.

✓ Demand Healthy Toys for Kids

Almost every toy commercially available is made, painted, or sealed with toxic chemicals. Fortunately, some companies still make high-quality toys from wood and other natural materials, but be aware that some wooden playground equipment uses pressure-treated lumber that's been chemically treated with very strong poisons or insecticides that can rub off on little hands or leach into the soil and waterways.

Look for play sets of cedar instead. And if you really want to make certain that any new wood needed was logged ethically, choose FSC (Forest Stewardship Council) certified lumber. Another choice is wood reclaimed or made from driftwood or "leftovers." Better yet, let your kids create their own toys from natural objects. Sticks can be turned into stilts, and trees can be excellent jungle gyms.

✓Look for Durable and Long Lasting

If you do buy a new toy, look at how it's made, and imagine if it will be around for a while. A good investment will outlast a child and allow you to gift it to another child rather than its ending up in a landfill. Here are some eco-friendly suppliers of kids' toys and other items:

- **www.blueberryforest.com**: Wooden games, puppets, dolls, puzzles

- **www.chinaberry.com**: Children's books about nature and the environment

- **www.hearthsong.com**: Natural toys since 1983

- **www.willowtreetoys.com**: Waldorf school toys

- **www.ostheimertoys.com**: Wooden toys and figures often used in Waldorf schools

- **www.fairtradesports.com**: Fair-trade footballs, soccer balls, volleyballs, and more

- **www.reusablebags.com**: Reusable lunch bags and juice or water bottles

- **www.oasischild.com**: Highly researched eco-conscious and open-ended toys

- **www.novanatural.com**: Wide variety of natural products that are conducive to creative and wholesome living

- **www.thewoodenwagon.com**: Natural European wooden toys, nontoxic art supplies from Stockmar, costumes from Fairy Finery, and many other products designed to foster creative play in children

- **www.hazelnutkids.com**: Large selection of natural, healthy toys, including European- and American-made toys; the company plants a tree for each product that's purchased

✓*Stick with Natural and Organic Instead of Synthetic*

Most conventionally grown cotton uses some of the most toxic pesticides and environmentally unfriendly fertilizers, which leave trace amounts in finished products. You can find organic-cotton clothing, bedding, blankets, and toys.

- **www.kidalog.net**: Canadian company offering more than 3,000 items

- **www.oasischild.com**: Organic, sustainable, and earth conscious; made in the USA

In addition to cotton, you can find organic wool, hemp, and linen used in everything from socks to stuffed animals and even lunch bags. Here are some places to start:

- **www.speesees.com**: Organic clothing

- **www.bamboosa.com**: Bamboo-fabric clothing

- **www.obliorganics.com**: Organic clothing for babies, toddlers, and doggies

- **www.katequinnorganics.com**: Stylish apparel made from 100 percent certified-organic cotton

- **www.oscarandbelle.com**: Organic and natural items that are not only good for babies' health and the environment (and are produced ethically), but they're also fun and timeless

✔Become PVC Free—Stay Away from #3 or "V" for Vinyl

PVC (polyvinyl chloride) has been used to make everything from shower curtains and raincoats to pacifiers and teething rings. Many PVC products can release brain-damaging lead and phthalates, which have been linked to both cancer and hormone problems. According to a PVC fact sheet compiled by the Healthy Building Network, "Dioxin (the most potent carcinogen known), ethylene dichloride and vinyl chloride are unavoidably created in production of PVC and can cause severe health problems." If PVC is incinerated, it releases carcinogenic dioxin and other contaminants into the air. With children's growing immune systems, play it safe and keep PVC out of their lives.

Green Bite

PVC is considered a hazardous waste by most communities, so it can't be dumped in a regular landfill. Find your local hazardous-waste site to dispose of it properly. If practical, you might want to mail the item back to the manufacturer to deal with, along with a note saying why PVC shouldn't be used in manufacturing, and that it should go the way of DDT in pesticide or mercury in felt hats.

✔Research the Ingredients

Manufacturers aren't required to prove their marketing and label claims. And sadly, many words such as *gentle* or *natural* are subjective and may not necessarily mean that they're healthy for kids or the environment. Remember to research ingredients and product safety on the Skin Deep Website: **www.cosmeticsdatabase.com**.

✓ *Look for Fragrance-Free Products*

Fragrances in children's soaps, conditioners, and bubble baths are almost always derived from synthetic chemicals and have been linked to asthma and other respiratory difficulties. Resources for fragrance-free products for kids include the Website **www.simplepurebaby.com**. This company offers a line of soaps, shampoos, and other items that contain no synthetic fragrances, harsh chemicals, or synthetic preservatives. Earth Mama Angel Baby developed natural products to support pregnancy and the birth process. Seventh Generation, Pampers, and others make unscented baby wipes and cloth wipes.

✓ *Baby-Powder Alternatives*

Conventional baby powders contain talc, which can be a carcinogen when inhaled. In fact, the FDA reported that the majority of brands of talc contained asbestos. Powders may also contain chemical fragrance and dyes. Natural cornstarch and potato flour work wonderfully as a baby or grown-up powder. (Refer to the recipe for these natural powders in Chapter 3.) Also check out **www.farmaesthetics.com** for a product called "Body Dust."

✓ *Fluoride-Free and SLS-Free Toothpaste*

Fluoride helps prevent cavities, but it can be harmful if swallowed. High doses may cause staining on teeth and may also affect the nervous system. For children under two, the American Dental Association recommends fluoride-free toothpastes. Also look for ones that are free of sodium lauryl sulfate (SLS). It's best to seek out eco-friendly brands that don't need warning labels like conventionally made toothpastes.

- **www.tomsofmaine.com**: Children's fluoride-free and SLS-free toothpastes.

- **www.jason-natural.com**: Their all-natural Tea Tree Toothpaste contains no fluoride or SLS.

- Other brands in the safer range include Weleda, Auromère, and Homeodent.

✓ *Cloth, Disposable, or Hybrid Diapers?*

Disposable diapers pile up in landfills and don't decompose for many years, perhaps even hundreds. Cloth diapers are reusable, but they take energy and water to wash, dry, and transport them. Hybrids such as Bummis and gDiapers use biodegradable, flushable inner liners and reusable and washable outer covers. Toss the liner in the toilet and the cover in the washing machine. Unfortunately, the covers contain chemical-laden gels that, when flushed, can end up in waterways. They are also much harsher on little tushes.

The experts at Oasis Child (**www.oasischild .com**) recommend using cloth diapers as often as you can and hybrids when traveling. Organic-cotton cloth diapers never wind up in a landfill and can be passed on after use (if properly cared for), or reused as the softest dust rag you'll ever own.

Other alternatives include:

- **www.jilliansdrawers.com**: A natural-parenting resource center offering a wide variety of cloth diapers and diapering accessories

- **www.bummis.com**: Biodegradable, flushable diapers with reusable liners

- **www.gdiapers.com**: Plastic-free, flushable liners with breathable cotton pants

- **www.diaperjungle.com**: A wealth of links and articles so that you can do your own research

✓*Shampoos and Conditioners*

As I've mentioned, many shampoos contain DEA, a product that over time can reformulate with other ingredients to create carcinogens. Look for products without fragrances, preservatives, or any of the toxins listed in the Green Bite at the end of this chapter. Here are some better options for little ones:

- Baby Cakes Organic Therapeutic Shampoos
- Aubrey Organics Natural Baby & Kids Shampoo

- Dr. Bronner's Baby Mild Liquid Soap
- Earth Mama Angel Baby

✓ *Antibacterial Hand Sanitizers*

There is overwhelming evidence that antibacterial hand soaps cause more harm than good because they kill beneficial bacteria as well as the bad stuff. They may also help create superstrains of bacteria that are resistant to antibiotics. Avoid hand sanitizers that contain the ingredient triethanolamine, which can damage kidneys and liver.

✓ *Bubble Bath*

Baths are healthy, calming, and fun experiences for babies and kids. The challenge is that most commercial bubble baths contain toxins, synthetic fragrances, and often DEA. Children are much more sensitive than adults, and the FDA has received numerous complaints ranging from skin rashes to infections from the exposure to certain ingredients in conventionally made bubble bath. More information and eco-friendly products are available at **www.californiababy.com**. (You can also make your own healthy bubble bath; see the recipe in Chapter 3.)

✓ *Mayonnaise for Lice Treatment*

If kids do happen to catch the little buggers, try a greener solution rather than poisoning your tot's scalp with chemical-filled medicinal shampoos.

Try smothering the bugs with mayonnaise under a shower cap before bedtime and then washing hair thoroughly in the morning.

✓ Demand Healthier Food at Schools

Vending machines at many schools still dispense sugar-filled candy, junk food, and sodas. And for some school districts, the income from the vending machines is a revenue source for the school. If this is an issue at your school, gather support from other parents and petition the school district or PTA to put healthy food in both the vending machines and the lunch counter, if there is one. You can find more information on this issue at:

- **www.cspinet.org/schoolfoods**: The Center for Science in the Public Interest (CSPI) promotes the benefits of good nutrition and physical activity for kids.

- **www.healthcollaborative.net/assets/ pdf/vendingcriteria.pdf**: Provides healthy vending-machine guidelines.

- **www.greenliving.suite101.com**: Offers tips to green your kids.

- **www.oasischild.com**: Carries goodie bags, a full line of organic alternatives to plastic bags, as well as reusable and non-toxic water bottles, lunch kits, and bamboo flatware.

✓ Sunscreen

The jury is still out, but many feel that it's the toxic ingredients in sunscreens that we absorb through our skin—more than the sun—that contribute to the increase in skin cancers. See Chapter 3 for more information and healthy recommendations.

Green Bite
Avoid the following ingredients . . .

- *SLS (Sodium Lauryl Sulfate):* Can result in eye damage, irritations, and skin rashes. SLS can penetrate children's eyes and prevent them from developing properly; it may also cause cataracts in adults.

- *BHA*: Banned in the EU; can cause skin depigmentation.

- *Boric acid:* Avoid using on infants or damaged skin.

- *2-Bromo-2-Nitropropane-1,3-diol (Bronopol):* Allergen and irritant.

- *Ceteareth and PEG:* Impurities that are possible carcinogens.

- *DMDM Hydantoin:* Allergen and irritant.

- *Fluoride:* Neurotoxic agent; high doses can stain teeth.

- *Oxybenzone:* Allergy in sunlight; possible carcinogen.

- *Sodium borate:* Avoid using on infants or damaged skin.

- *Triclosan:* Linked to thyroid problems.

- *Triethanolamine:* Allergen and irritant, especially for liver and kidneys; possible carcinogen.

- *1,4-Dioxane:* Petroleum-derived contaminant considered a probable human carcinogen by the EPA and a definite animal carcinogen by the National Toxicology Program.

CHAPTER 8

GREEN YOUR PETS

As a kid, I always loved watching *Lassie* episodes when the heroic collie would run for help to save her owner's life. In October 1998, a woman from Pennsylvania had a real-life *Lassie* experience . . . except her heroic rescue story didn't involve a collie.

The account was published in the *Pittsburgh Post-Gazette:* A couple was enjoying their vacation home by Lake Erie, and one morning the husband left for a day of fishing. While home alone, his wife suddenly felt a sharp pain and collapsed on the bedroom floor. She was unable to move and could barely call out for help. Their American Eskimo dog began barking, apparently trying to draw attention. But it was to no avail.

That's when the couple's very large Vietnamese potbellied pig sprang into action. LuLu squeezed her way out through the doggie door, pushed open the gate into the yard, and ran out to the street. Witnesses stated that Lulu waited until a car approached, and then she ran into the middle of the street and laid her large round body down. One motorist stopped, but later said that he was afraid to get out because he was so unsure of the creature in the road.

A few more cars just drove around LuLu. As time passed, she returned to her master's side several times, only to leave again to seek help. After 45 minutes, a man finally stopped his car and got out to see what was in the road. LuLu jumped up and led the man to the house, constantly turning back to make sure the Good Samaritan was still following her.

The motorist walked to the back door and shouted, "Your pig is distressed."

The woman inside yelled, "I'm in distress, too! Please call an ambulance!" When the ambulance arrived, LuLu tried to go to the hospital with them, but the medics gently relieved her of further duties for the day. Later the woman was told by her doctors that she'd suffered a heart attack, and if she had lain there another 15 minutes, she most likely would have died. The remaining years of her life were owed to LuLu.

We can't come close to creating machines that equal the skills and abilities of animals. Scientists are even studying animals that are able to perceive early warning signs for tsunamis and earthquakes. Dolphins have helped in numerous rescues and underwater tasks, and pigeons have been trained to spot orange life jackets of people who are lost at sea. The existence of animals is an incredible gift, and each species is invaluable in the tapestry of life on this planet.

> *"Until one has loved an animal,*
> *a part of one's soul remains unawakened."*
> — **Anatole France**

Make Green Easy

The unintended consequences of human actions are affecting the ability of many species to survive. By taking a few small steps and making better choices, we can take loving care of our own pets while also enhancing the lives of other members of the animal kingdom.

✓ *Spay or Neuter Your Pet*

More than 5,500 puppies and kittens (compared to 415 human babies) are born every hour in the United States.[1] Far too many of them end up in shelters or are euthanized. Spaying or neutering greatly increases the life span of your pet and avoids the possibility of unwanted offspring and the environmental, financial, and emotional impact of unwanted animals.

Green Bite

Spayed and neutered animals no longer need to roam to look for a mate. They stay home more and get into fewer fights. For males it reduces problems with territorial and sexual aggression, as well as spraying. For females, spaying decreases the chances of breast cancer (down to almost zero if spaying is done before the first heat cycle). In addition, spaying eliminates the heat cycle, mood swings, and visits from interested males in the neighborhood.

✓Adopt a Pet

Pet shelters are full of wonderful animals in need of a home. You'll also save money, as shelters typically charge only for licensing and spaying or neutering. Visit your local animal shelter or check out **www.petfinder.com**, **www.greyhoundgang .org**, or **www.craigslist.com**.

✓Avoid Junk Pet Food

Most canned pet food available at supermarkets contains the lowest grade of meat possible— labeled "4-D," which is a nice way of saying that the pet food was made from animals that were "dead, dying, disabled, or diseased."[2] Since nutrition is one of the key factors of health and resistance to disease, ideally, you want your pet's diet to be better than that.

✔ Share Food with Your Pet

Research has shown that dogs don't need all of the grain, soy, and low-quality meat in commercial dog foods.[3] Many owners have raised healthy dogs and cats into old age by feeding them a little of each day's household human fare. Make a little more meat loaf, chicken soup, green beans, or spinach when you cook for your family. Your pet just might live a longer, better life; and you'll be simplifying things while reducing the volume of all those metal pet-food cans that are made and trashed.

✔ Purchase Natural and Organic Pet Foods

Natural and organic pet foods are much healthier for your pet and the planet. They typically contain no 4-D meat, chemical fertilizers, antibiotics, or steroids, neither do they add any chemical additives, artificial preservatives, flavors, colors, or dyes. We all should eat so good! (**Note:** Transition your pet slowly to new foods.)

✔ Stay Away from Flea Collars

The Natural Resources Defense Council (NRDC) has stated that the pesticides used in flea collars, shampoos, dust, and dips pose a serious health risk, especially to pregnant women and children. "Flea collars create a toxic cloud around your animal 24 hours a day," asserts the NRDC.[4]

green your pets

Green Bite

The U.S. Environmental Protection Agency (EPA) didn't start to review the safety of pet products until 1996. There is a backlog of products waiting to be tested. So just because an item is on a store shelf, it doesn't mean that it has been tested or that you can assume it's safe for your pet.[5]

✔ Flea-Control Options

Frequent bathing, brushing pets regularly with a flea comb, inspecting for fleas, and vacuuming carpets and furniture regularly are all effective ways to help keep fleas at bay.

✔ Brewer's Yeast for Fleas

Mixing a teaspoon of Nutri-yeast or brewer's yeast into your pet's food every other day or so can help keep fleas away. Apparently, pets who consume it don't taste as good to fleas.

✔ Homemade Flea Collars

Adding the essential oil of citronella to an absorbent fabric collar can deter fleas. A pet's sense of smell is much more sensitive than a human's, so start with a single drop of 100 percent pure oil and see if your pet is happy with that. You can repeat it every few days, depending on your pet's sensitivity.

Place the oil on the outside of the collar so that it doesn't rub up against or irritate your pet's skin.

✓ Other Flea-Control Products

Recent flea-control products are insect-growth regulators (IGRs), which aren't pesticides but chemicals that affect the growth cycle of fleas. These include methoprene, fenoxycarb, pyriproxyfen, and the popular lufenuron (Program®). Check the warning labels for adverse effects or cautions—for example, most are not recommended for use in lactating female animals.

Alternatives also include new pesticide products, which are oils packaged by dosage in tubes (doses are determined by weight ranges). Two of these are fipronil (Frontline®) and imidacloprid (Advantage®). These medications are toxic to fleas; however, they're also toxic to some beneficial insects, marine life, and birds.

✓ Use Biodegradable Doggie Bags

Of course you pick up after your pooch, but do you use biodegradable bags so that your best friend's waste isn't mummified in plastic for a few hundred years in a landfill somewhere?

✓ Compost Pet Waste

If you have room in your backyard, you can bury a small plastic trash bin with the bottom cut out. Locate it away from your vegetable garden to prevent pathogens from making their way to your organic veggies. Composted pet waste should not be used on fruit or vegetable gardens, or on any other plants intended for human consumption. Check out the Doggie Dooley (**www.doggiedooley** **.com**). This company also sells a "super digester concentrate" for your backyard pet-waste digester.

Green Bite

The first animal methane digester in the U.S. is being built in San Francisco to turn the city's 6,500 tons of dog poop a year into compost, natural gas, and electricity.[6] Now that's thinking ahead!

✔ Choose Better Cat Litter

Instead of conventional clay litter, consider an eco-friendly option. Swheat Scoop is a wheat-based clumping cat litter that's made without clays and chemicals, and it's fragrance free and biodegradable. It's even flushable. Check it out at **www.swheatscoop.com**.

Green Bite

Not only is the bentonite clay used in many cat litters strip-mined and not eco-friendly in the way it's produced, but the clay also contains carcinogenic silica dust that can damage kitty's lungs. Bentonite is used in construction and to seal ponds from leaking. It swells up to 15 times its normal size and can clog your cat's intestines if ingested during grooming. Another unfriendly litter is the kind with "pearls" or "crystals" of silica. Silica sucks up moisture, and if it's digested, it can lead to dehydration or other health problems.[7]

✓ Use Natural Pet-Care and Cleaning Products

Toxic chemicals in pet shampoos aren't good for your furry friends or the planet. Many pet owners love Dr. Bronner's soaps because they're organic and biodegradable, and they step lightly on the earth. The eucalyptus-scented soaps contain a natural flea deterrent.

✓ Natural Pet Toys

Instead of plastic toys that are fossil-fuel based, go natural, get creative, and save some money. Pine cones (without the sap) make great kitty toys. A tree branch for playing fetch with Fido costs nothing. Scrap fabric and yarn that's headed for the trash can easily be transformed into pet toys. All these choices save oil by not needing to be manufactured, packaged, trucked, and shipped halfway around the earth.

✓ *Support Sustainable-Product Manufacturers*

For items you can't make, go for the most earth-friendly, locally made products. You can find hemp collars and leashes that will outlast most other natural fibers, pet beds made of organic cotton or even recycled plastic bottles, and cat scratching posts made from recycled cardboard. See **www.planetdog.com**.

✓ *Stuffed Animals May Be Better Than Live Ones*

Unless you're really willing to commit to the care and responsibility it takes to raise livestock, it's probably best not to buy those Easter chicks, no matter how cute they are or how much your youngster wants one. (The same applies to Easter bunnies.) Little chicks grow up to be chickens that lay eggs, and that can be a great thing if you're prepared to care for them in an adequate pen or safe yard.

Check with local codes, because some cities don't allow chickens or may limit how many you can keep. Also be forewarned that it's difficult to tell hens from roosters when they're young, and the morning behavior of growing roosters may make you none too popular with your neighbors.

✓ *Safe Deicer for Cold Climates*

If you live in a cold climate and need to de-ice your sidewalks, consider a pet- and child-safe product such as Safe Paw. The warnings on traditional salt used to melt ice indicate that it's dangerous for animals and children. Check **www.safepaw.com** for more information.

✓ *Grow Your Own Kitty Grass and Catnip*

Cats love to chew on grass, but many indoor cats never get the chance. Catnip is a natural, non-addictive mood enhancer that most kitties love. You can easily grow both grass and catnip indoors in a pot or outside on a deck or patio. Organic catnip seeds are available at many nurseries or online. For kitty grass, pick up organic wheat berries from a health-food store. They're typically used for sprouting. Plant them in potting soil in a small container. In a few weeks, your cats will have their own mini cat lawn.

✓ *Better Bedding*

For small pets such as hamsters and gerbils, traditional bedding has been cedar or pine shavings. Look for alternatives including recycled newspaper; straw pellets (straw is annually renewable as opposed to trees, which may take many years to reach maturity); and AirLite, a recycled-cardboard bedding.

✓ *Only Approved Exotics*

Turtles, birds, snakes, lizards, and other exotics can make good pets, especially for folks who are allergic to fur or dander. But make sure you can provide the correct environment and the means to give them a good home. Also be sure that any exotic pets were bred in captivity and not poached from a natural environment.

Green Bite

To make certain the exotic animal you're interested in isn't an endangered species, check with the Convention on International Trade in Endangered Species of Wild Fauna and Flora. Thankfully, their Web address is much simpler than their name: **www.cites.org**.

PART II

GREEN YOUR HOME

CHAPTER 9

GREEN YOUR BEDROOM

We spend about a third of our lives in the bedroom. This means that transforming our bedrooms into healthful sanctuaries where our bodies, minds, and spirits can truly rest and be restored is one of the most effective steps we can take toward our own well-being. Our world has become more and more contaminated with chemical toxins that build up in our bodies and tax our immune systems; but a safe, clean, and natural bedroom can act as a daily cleanser and rejuvenator.

In creating a bedroom sanctuary, we open the way for the daily renewal of the connection to our personal reservoirs of energy and peak functioning. During our hours of rest, we lie in our beds, trusting and accepting our environment. All we're doing is simply breathing, yet we want to inhale the cleanest air possible. In a green bedroom, as we close our eyes at night the last image we see can be one of beauty, and the last impression we sense can be of the wholeness of the room that's enveloping and protecting us as we drift off to sleep. Waking up in the morning, we reenter that wholeness and beauty in preparation for the new day ahead. Our first conscious breath can be taken with relaxed and joyous confidence, as we bask in the security and warmth of our familiar, all-natural surroundings.

To support and enhance your sleeping and waking states, wise eco-choices for your bedroom are imperative. These can determine both your depth of comfort at night and the effectiveness of your relationships with family members or at your workplace during the day. Perhaps more than any other single room in the home, the bedroom offers the greatest harvest, as you plant the seeds for a green return to a more natural lifestyle.

There are healthy alternatives available for everything from paints and floor coverings to sheets and mattresses. Here are some basics that should get you started on the path toward a healthier lifestyle with more clarity, energy, and focus.

Make Green Easy

✔ *Start with Healthy Sheets*

A great place to start on the path toward creating your healing bedroom retreat is with your pillow cases, sheets, and comforter covers. Go with organic cotton, bamboo, or linen sheets; and consider organic flannel for warmer winter nights. Many large retailers such as Macy's, Bed Bath & Beyond, Pottery Barn, and even Target now carry beautiful organic sheets at reasonable prices. You'll be surrounding yourself in the restful vibration of nature, supporting organic farmers, and lessening the use and impact of chemical fertilizers and pesticides.

Green Bite

Avoid petroleum-based polyester sheets or no-iron sheets. The resins used in no-iron fabrics are considered toxic, and washing them can never eliminate the resins completely.

✔ *Comforters*

Rather than synthetic poly-filled comforters, consider a natural option like goose down or organic wool. They may be more expensive than what you're used to, but with proper care they'll last for generations. For those who are allergic to wool, organic-cotton comforters and blankets are a good option, and they're more affordable than wool or down.

✓*Healthful Pillows*

Every night you nestle your nose into your pillow and usually don't give a thought to what you may be breathing in. But if you want to make sure you don't stay awake at night wondering what's in your pillow, pick up an organic-cotton, wool, or natural-latex pillow that guarantees you're not ingesting any harmful pesticides or chemical residues. When the weather is nice, air your pillows out in the sun to kill any hidden mold that might be growing.

✓*Mattress Matters*

— *Organic-cotton mattresses.* Most mattresses sold in developed countries contain chemicals (many untested) such as herbicides, fire retardants, formaldehyde, pesticides, and stain-resistant solvents. Look for organic-cotton mattresses and futons that are free of toxins.

— *Organic-wool mattresses.* Wool is naturally fire resistant and probably won't have fire-retardant chemicals. But unless your mattress is pure organic wool, it might contain residual pesticides used on sheep to control insects. Go with organic wool to be sure and safe.

— *Natural-latex mattresses.* Although natural-latex beds may be the most expensive initially, they can turn out to be the best value because of how long they last. They've been around since the 1920s. Sears sold an all-natural latex mattress back in the 1950s called the Harvest House bed, and many that received moderate use as guest beds are still intact—40 to 50 years later. Several manufacturers offer a 20-year warranty on natural-latex mattresses.

Be aware, however. The majority of latex beds are made from synthetic latex (or a combination of natural and synthetic), a petrochemical compound with no healthful advantages. Natural latex comes from Mother Nature's own rubber tree and has many benefits over synthetics, including the fact that dust mites are unable to grow in natural latex, natural rubber is a renewable resource, and a natural-latex mattress has no flame-retardant chemicals or toxic outgassing. (In this case, *outgassing* refers to the slow release of potentially toxic gases that are trapped inside a mattress made from synthetic materials.)

✓ Play It Safe with Electromagnetic Frequencies

Most of us have driven under a high power line and noticed that our radio signal was disrupted or distorted. This is due to the electromagnetic field (EMF) generated from the power lines. This same energy can affect our bodies, as we are bioelectric beings. Many researchers and scientists feel that exposure to raised frequencies can be an important factor in determining whether we're obtaining good, restful sleep.

Look around your bedroom. Is there a clock radio on the nightstand near your mattress? Do you have a TV or stereo nearby? Do you use an electric blanket? All of these can contribute to elevating the EMFs that silently and quietly affect your mind and body.

I've tested EMF levels personally with a specialized meter and found one instance in which a clock radio was very "EMF hot." This high frequency radiated to the metal-coil springs of the mattress and box spring, lifting the entire bed to an EMF level far exceeding what's considered safe. Here are some easy fixes you can do in your own home:

- Remove any electrical appliances or electronics from within six feet of your bed.

- Use a battery-operated clock.

- Kill any power vampires in the bedroom. (See Chapter 19 for more information.)

- Retire any electric blankets. (These are very EMF hot.) Or, invest in new DC (direct current) electric blankets with much lower EMF levels.

- Contact a baubiologist (one who studies how buildings impact life and the living environment) if you want to do more work on lowering EMF levels.

- Check out **www.lessemf.com** for products that shield or block EMFs.

Green Bite

"The government of Sweden funded an official, massive study of the effects of electric fields from overhead power lines on 500,000 people over a period of 25 years and found overwhelming evidence that electric fields generated cancer in children at four times the normal rate and tripled the rate in adults. Sweden lists elevated electromagnetic fields (EMF) as Class 2 Carcinogens, right along with tobacco."

— www.think-aboutit.com/
energy/pwr_line.htm

✓*Pay Attention to Details*

Pay attention to everything you allow into your sacred bedroom space, including the following:

- Are all the soaps, personal products, and cleaners used in your bedroom nontoxic and eco-friendly?

- Is the bedroom furniture old enough to have outgassed any toxins?

- Is the flooring easily kept clean—that is, could it be harboring mold, toxins, or other nasties?

- When you need new towels, consider going organic.

- Are any candles free from toxic fragrances? Beeswax is best. Beeswax candles also burn about five times longer than paraffin candles and give off healthful negative ions. Pertoleum-based paraffinic candles are like miniature diesel motors that add soot to your indoor air and eventually to your lungs.

- Are there any phantom loads ("leaking" electricity from electronics or appliances left on) or distracting lights that you can eliminate?

- Are all draperies made from healthy fabrics?

- Has the lighting been looked at for efficiency and aesthetics? Quartz torchiere lights are not only energy inefficient and add unwanted heat and expense, but they've also caused numerous fires when fabrics touch the bulbs.

- Is artwork made from natural materials (to avoid outgassing of petrochemical products)?

CHAPTER 10
GREEN YOUR WATER

Tres Piedras is a little crossroads town about 40 miles north of Taos, New Mexico, as the crow flies. The name comes from three magnificent rock outcroppings, each bigger than ten houses. They sit by themselves, peering over the expanse of sage, piñon, and cedar trees that roll outward for hundreds of miles in most directions. Many years ago my first wife, Heidi, and I bought ten acres of raw land in this wild mountain valley with dreams of creating a small retreat for ourselves.

TP, as the locals refer to the town, is located at roughly 8,000 feet in elevation, so you have to watch your exertion the first few days when you arrive. You can get winded by just walking too fast. The quiet takes some getting used to as well. The town isn't much to speak of. There's one gas station, the post office, a diner . . . and that's about it. The diner looks like someone just beamed it up from New York City and plopped it down in the sagebrush. It's one of those art-deco 1920s types with chrome-curved everything.

The vast landscape is peppered with black-volcanic rock strewn about under the cedar and piñon trees. The story is that they're from a volcanic eruption some 100,000 years past. No developers, bulldozers, or even pickaxes have touched the land in all that time; and blackened baseballs and beach balls lodge partly buried right where they landed over the years.

The plants that survive here are a bizarre mix of the toughest ones from the clash in various bioregions—the high desert, savannah, and mountain ranges. In spring, bright orange Indian paintbrush, purple lupin flowers, and sage fill in the bare spots between the rocks. There's the occasional small delicate cactus that makes its way up from the valley floor hiding under the arms of a hundred-year-old piñon tree.

The first time I drove out from California to spend some time on the land, I slept under the heavens each night in a down sleeping bag. The stars are some of the brightest and most awe inspiring that I've ever had the honor to witness. It was sometimes difficult to fall asleep with all that excitement going on overhead. Constellations stood out brilliantly, and from one end of the horizon to the other, I could see the edge of the Milky Way so thick with stars it almost looked solid.

On my third day, huge thunderheads rolled in from the north, and at sunset I experienced my first New Mexico monsoon. I hung a blue plastic tarp in an attempt to stay dry and another one to catch the rain and funnel it into a large tub. I tied the tarp corners and sides to a few of the large rocks close by. However, with monsoons also come winds. By nightfall, my tarp had turned into a giant flapping bird with the single mission of keeping me awake.

I survived. A day later, the clouds moved south past our little mountain, and the sun came peeking through. I crawled out from under my shelter and surveyed the land. Mud holes had replaced the dry hollows, and my 55-gallon tub was nearly full of rainwater. That "gift from the gods" would go to good use during the next few weeks. Between mixing mud for concrete and staying clean, the water didn't last long. I almost wished for more rain so I wouldn't have to bring in a water truck.

Some 15 years have passed since those first nights spent under the stars. We now have a small warm cabin with a woodstove, and we vacation there when we're in need of a respite from the hustle and bustle of Southern California. A lot has changed for me personally since then, but not much has changed on the land. Those 15 years are a flash, a fleeting instant, for Mother Nature. We still see elk, coyote, and antelope. The Indian paintbrush and lupin still celebrate the coming of spring, and we still receive our water from the heavens.

I've realized that when you live off the water you catch from your roof, you become quite proficient at making every drop count. In our cabin, the kitchen sink is plumbed to water the outside plants. Our shower water goes back to the earth, we brush our teeth like we do when we're camping in nature, and we still even use our outhouse. We wouldn't think of wasting great rainwater for flushing waste.

Make Green Easy

✓ Fix Faucet and Toilet Leaks

A leaky faucet can drip 20 gallons a day, and a leaky toilet can let two to five times that much get away. Leave an empty glass under a faucet overnight to see if you're letting water and money go down the drain. For toilets, put a couple drops of food coloring in the tank. Wait an hour, and see if any color has leaked into the bowl. If you've got tinted water in the bowl, you've got a leak that needs repairing.

Green Bite

You can check your entire home to see if there are any water leaks. Read your water meter before you retire at night and again in the morning. If you haven't irrigated or used any water and the meter doesn't indicate the exact same number, there's a leak somewhere.

✓ *Install Low-Flow Showerheads*

Change any high-flow showerheads to the newer low-flow types. Before the 1990s, some showerheads had flow rates of 5.5 gallons per minute! The ones available today will give you an invigorating shower while using only half or a third of the water as the old designs. For an investment of about $10 or less, you can save $40 to $80 a year on water bills. Look for the solid-brass or bronze heads with chrome plating. Skip over plastic ones because they don't last as long. Depending on how you heat your water (solar, natural gas, propane, or electricity), you can save energy costs and carbon emissions at the same time. See **www.NewLeafAmerica.com.**

✓ *Add Faucet Aerators*

Faucet aerators add air to the water stream to provide more rinse-off power with much less water. The majority of faucets produced today will come with an aerator, but older ones may not, or the screens in old aerators may be rusted out.

✓ *Be Water Wise*

Changing small habits, such as brushing your teeth without leaving the water running, can save two to three gallons of pure fresh water each time you brush your pearly whites. Also try filling the sink basin for washing or shaving instead of leaving it running.

green your water

Wash fruits and vegetables, and rinse dishes in a tub in your sink. Then pour the water you've saved on your plants or in your garden. In addition, don't run water to thaw meat or frozen foods. Defrost food overnight in the refrigerator instead.

✓ Compost Instead of Using a Garbage Disposal

Save money and water by easing up on when you use your garbage disposal. Whenever you turn on the garbage disposal, water runs down the drain and electricity is used. Composting is a much greener option and gives you great fertilizer for your garden. (See Chapter 12, which is devoted to composting.)

✓ Use Cold Water Before Hot

If you're rinsing dishes or cleaning the sink, using cold water will save the electricity or fuel that's being used to heat your water. Unless, of course, you get all your hot water from solar in the first place.

✓ Purchase Smart Timers and Drip Systems for Irrigation

Along with shrinking our lawns, adding drip irrigation that puts water directly on plants instead of spraying it into the air can cut your water bill and save electricity. Many communities use vast amounts of power just to move water. In

California, pumping water and sewage accounts for 19 percent of all the electricity used.[1]

Another newer technology that conserves water is a smart timer. These sense humidity and temperature from satellite weather data to adjust and deliver the right amount of water to your garden, so there are no sprinklers running in the rain. Smart timers can be set to water in the early morning or late afternoon to avoid water loss from evaporation.

✓ *Install High-Efficiency or Dual-Flush Toilets*

Toilets have gone from using 7 gallons of water per flush to 5 gallons, then 3, and now by law, 1.6 gallons (some new high-efficiency models use just 1.3 gallons or less). If you have a toilet that was installed before 1992, replacing it will save thousands of gallons a year. Some of the first low-flow models worked better than others, but today's high-efficiency ones save water without any trade-offs in flushing power. In addition, several companies manufacture dual-flush toilets, which use only a half flush (0.8 gallons) when needed.

✓ *Use Refillable Water Bottles and a Home Filter*

Install a good-quality water filter and pick up a refillable water bottle or two. I prefer the stainless-steel bottles, which are easy to find online or at health-food stores. There are numerous water filters available today. Research some Websites or consumer magazines and purchase a durable water filter, preferably one with replaceable cartridges. Forty percent of all bottled water sold started out as tap water that has been filtered and bottled.[2]

Green Bite

Plastic disposable bottles create an enormous environmental toll. It's estimated that 1.5 million barrels of oil are used every year to manufacture the 70 million bottles of water consumed each day in the U.S. And according to the Container Recycling Institute, 86 percent of plastic water bottles used in the U.S. isn't recycled. Those thin plastic bottles actually take over 1,000 years to break down in a landfill.

✓ Run Dishwashers and Washing Machines Full

Another energy-saving habit is to run your dishwasher only when it's full—no half loads. Many new dishwashers are very good at cleaning dishes that have only been scraped (not prerinsed), and some include a prerinse cycle when heavy cleaning is needed. Experiment with different full loads and see what works best for you.

Newer washing machines have options for smaller loads when needed. Otherwise, wash loads as full as possible.

✓*Lighten Up on the Red Meat*

Red meat may not seem like it relates to water, but raising livestock is among the most demanding industries on the global water supply. Lighten up on your red-meat intake and you'll be lessening your eco-impact. Factory-livestock farms use water to grow the grain fed to animals and of course, to provide them with drinking water. However, antibiotics, hormones, chemicals, fertilizers, and the pesticides used on feed crops—along with pollution from animal waste—all end up in our natural water systems. So the less meat you eat, the less pollution will end up in our water sources.

Green Bite

About 70 percent of the Amazon rainforests have been cleared and used for grazing.

✓*Use a Broom Instead of a Hose for Sweeping*

This is another change of habit that will save water and keep our oceans, rivers, and lakes cleaner. When we wash down our sidewalks and driveways, we push gunk such as motor oil, transmission fluid, and brake linings downstream. Much of the downstream runoff ends up in our watercourses and blue belts (lakes, oceans, and rivers).

✓ Use Water Twice

Gray water is water that's been used once—for instance, from a kitchen sink or shower—and then is used a second time for landscaping. Practicing this has become more and more important, especially in the Southwest and other areas that experience droughts. Arizona has one of the best and most adopted gray-water systems in the U.S.

Often the kitchen sink is next to an exterior wall, which makes it pretty simple to direct that water outside to your garden. Most state laws require that gray water be delivered below ground to prevent any pathogens from becoming airborne. This can be accomplished simply by using an upside-down, unglazed ceramic pot with a gravel pit below. For great information on this, see **www.oasis design.net** or **www.greywaterguerrillas.com**.

✓ Catch the Rain

Rain catchment has been used historically as the purest source of water for countless regions and peoples. Today, New Mexico, Texas, and Hawaii are joined by New Zealand, Australia, and most of South America in being set up to catch and store thousands of gallons of water at each home for use during the dry seasons.

Check your local laws. You can get started in most areas with a simple rain barrel—except in Colorado where it's illegal to catch rainwater or snow! Here are a few more resources:

- www.rain-barrel.net
- www.rainbarrelguide.com
- www.harvesth2o.com

Storing water in the earth is even more effective than catchment for irrigation needs. Sculpting your site to catch and store rain in the top few feet of soil will hold much more water than tanks and stretch out your growing season longer. For more information on rainwater harvesting, even in drylands, visit **www.rainwaterharvesting.com**.

Green Bite

Asphalt-shingle roofs leach toxic petrochemical poisons into rainwater and are not suitable to catch water for consumption. When it's time to replace your roof, go with a nontoxic and longer-lasting material such as metal. According to the California Integrated Waste Management Board, "Approximately 11 million tons of waste asphalt roofing shingles are generated in the U.S. per year."[3] And because asphalt-shingle roofs must be replaced after 15 or 20 years, they end up being one of the most expensive options when you think about long-term savings.

✓*Support Car Washes That Conserve Water*

Washing your car at home uses about 500 gallons on average, according to the EPA.[4] In comparison, the International Carwash Association claims that a commercial car wash uses only about 32 gallons of water per car.[5]

You can also try waterless car-washing products at home that don't use a drop and can be wiped off without needing to be rinsed. Eco Touch, Freedom, and Lucky Earth are a few eco-friendly brands to look for.

✓ Buy Water-Efficient Appliances

When you need new appliances, buy ones that are energy efficient and conserve water, such as front-loading washing machines and low-water-use dishwashers. Look for Energy Star models, which use less water and electricity, and don't forget to use nontoxic detergents and soaps to do the job.

✓ Fix the Wait for Hot Water

If you have to wait a long time for hot water to get to a faucet or shower, here are a few things you can do to fix the problem while also benefiting the environment:

• Insulate your water heater and pipes.

• Save the water in a shower or basin with a bucket and reuse it.

• Consider a small "on demand" electric heater for a bath faucet that's positioned a long way from the water heater. You won't have any wait or wasted water, but you will use electricity. (In this case, you need to figure out which is more valuable in your situation: electricity, water, or the fuel to heat your water.)

- Add a recirculation pump that will bring the hot water to that farthest fixture right away. The pumps use a bit of electricity, so once again, you'll have to weigh the advantages. Metlund Hot Water D'MAND system is one brand that can be retrofitted without adding plumbing return lines.

- Install a "ladybug" water saver on showerheads. This little valve senses the water temperature and slows to a trickle when the shower gets hot. Flip a switch and you have full pressure. Saves waiting and testing to see if the water is hot or not. See **www.NewLeafAmerica.com.**

CHAPTER 11
GREEN YOUR GARDEN

In 1969, I was 13 years old and my dad was the head systems engineer for the Sealab III project. This was an undersea lab, Jacques Cousteau style, where divers and scientists would stay down for weeks or months trying to discover ways to feed the world or make medicines, all from the ocean. They even had a trained porpoise that delivered supplies to the underwater lab! I was at the inauguration of the Sealab and even got to go on board. For a kid, it was pretty cool to see walls filled with hundreds of shiny round gauges and port-holes to look out from. The whole exterior was covered with hoses, pipes, and tanks. It was an exciting time, and Dad was filled with hope. This was just the kind of project he'd dreamed of.

But one day my father came home, didn't say a word, and went straight to bed. My mom followed him into their bedroom, and they stayed there speaking quite softly for a long time. When Mom finally came out, she told us kids that one of the divers on the Sealab had drowned. The project was shut down a few months later, and my dad was laid off for the first time in his life. He slipped into a depression that would last for several months.

Interestingly, those 12 months without much money may have been the greatest year my family ever had together. I think it may have been one of my mom's best years, too. She came into her own that summer. After a couple weeks with no other job opportunities for my dad, we sat down for a family powwow. Mom took charge: "All right, we're all going to pitch in and work together. This isn't a problem. I'll show you how we did this on the farm, but first we're going to dig up the whole backyard." We all looked at each other and didn't know what to think—we had a huge backyard.

The next day, with Mom in charge, Dad rented a rototiller and started churning up our perfect-ly good lawn. Then we all helped pull out every clump of grass, shake off the dirt, and pile it up. Little by little more of the dark brown soil was ex-posed. Mom was all excited; you'd think she'd just won the lottery. She kept lifting clumps of dirt and crumbling it between her hands, letting it fall back and blend with all the rest. "You don't know how lucky we are. This is great dirt!" Then she'd start into one of her stories that always began the same way: "Back on the farm, why, we'd have to. . . ." She would effortlessly slip into another place and time while continuing whatever work she was doing.

Mom was the oldest of 13 children, a mixed breed of pioneer descendants and Native American Cherokee. As a teenager, she was sent to live with her grandparents and help on their farm. They had no electricity or running water. The few meager dollars they did earn from raising cotton would go to buying staples that had to last the entire year. This was many years before strip malls or Internet shopping. They grew corn for corn bread, and their milk and butter came from their own cows. They fished and hunted when they could. They reused or modified everything they needed on the farm.

Mom taught us all how to make and can preserves. Old peanut-butter and mayonnaise jars were filled with jams from our plum and peach trees. We melted wax to seal the top with a little piece of string to grab when you were ready to dig in. We grew squash, zucchini, peas, beans, greens, melons, and tomatoes that were mouth watering. Mom would fill old milk cartons with vegetables and freeze them for the winter. She'd never take the time to label what was in them, so on more than one occasion we had squash for a few days in a row. But we always had plenty of food for the eight of us from that backyard garden.

My mom's knowledge was needed and valued. She was the leader, and she took care of her family. She was also passing down what had been taught to her by her parents and grandparents. She was teaching my siblings and me basic life skills that had allowed humankind to flourish for thousands of years.

— green your garden

Make Green Easy

"Recall that whatever lofty things you might accomplish today, you will do them only because you first ate something that grew out of dirt."
— **Barbara Kingsolver**

Brought up-to-date, what follows are the type of principles my mom embraced.

✓*Shrink Your Lawn*

Since lawns are often made of only a few types of plants that most animals don't consume, they don't provide a lot of value for wildlife. Replacing grass lawn with native wildflowers, bushes, and trees provides the food, shelter, and cover that help maintain healthy, natural ecosystems.

Green Bite

The EPA estimates that the total amount of residential lawn in the United States covers about 40 million acres, making turfgrass the nation's largest irrigated crop area—without any food to show for it.

✓*Add More Natives*

Native plants, the ones that lived in your area before European settlers came, have adapted to the climate and wildlife of your bioregion. They provide important food and shelter for migratory birds and native wildlife—for example, the beautiful milkweed plant is the only food that a monarch-butterfly caterpillar eats. Natives typically require less water than nonnatives and are hardier.

✓ Go Organic with Fertilizers

All plants need nitrogen, phosphate, and potassium. Organic fertilizer is simply a fertilizer that takes these nutrients from organic matter such as manure, green waste, bone, or kelp. Synthetic chemical fertilizers are processed from petroleum or petrogasses and deliver their nutrients in a quick-release, water-soluble form that leaches into waterways and is harmful to marine life.

✓ Say No to Chemical Pesticides

The use of chemical pesticides can have un-intended effects on the environment. More than half of American home owners regularly douse their yards with pesticides, some of which, recent research indicates, may cause reproductive harm to wildlife *and* people. More than 98 percent of sprayed insecticides and 95 percent of herbicides reach a destination other than their target. The U.S. Geological Survey announced in 2007 that "pesticides were found in almost all waterways and in some drinking-water systems." We don't need that when there are better options.

✓ *Try Biological Pest Control*

Ladybugs and praying mantises are two beneficial insects that can clear aphids and other pests from plants. Certain plants and herbs contain natural pest deterrents and can be planted in your garden to add beauty and keep bugs away naturally. There are also plant-based insecticides that aren't harmful to humans or the environment. If pests are a big problem, ask about environmentally sensitive alternatives at your local nursery. More information is available at **www.gardenguides .com/pests/tips/herbal.asp**.

✓ *Invest in Fruit Trees*

Harvesting your own organic fruit is a delight, and you'll be using the least possible amount of fossil fuel to transport those delicious morsels from grove to home. Look for native varieties that flourish in your climate zone first. If space is a challenge, go with dwarf trees, which are only three to four feet around and can do quite well in containers. Semidwarfs are another option for small yards.

✓ *Plant Some Veggies*

There can be so much joy and reward in picking the perfect vine-ripened tomato or fresh salad fixings from your own garden. Even apartment dwellers can experience this by cultivating a few potted plants. And just like getting fruit from your own tree, homegrown vegetables offer you with the lowest eco-impact from transportation.

✔ *Use Heirloom Seeds*

Today's factory farms use mostly hybrid seeds that produce consistent but sterile plants—that is, the seeds won't grow another plant. Heirlooms, on the other hand, have been around for a long time. Some heirloom varieties are hundreds of years old and possibly even date back before recorded history. Heirlooms have adapted over time to whatever climate and soil they were grown in, often making them resistant to diseases, local pests, and weather swings. They're also some of the most interesting-looking produce you'll find.

✔ *Promote Good Soil*

Every experienced gardener knows that the secret to a great garden is having good organic soil. Here's another secret: good soil is a living being. It needs to breathe, retain moisture, and provide a food supply to all of the plants it's nourishing; as well as to beneficial insects such as earthworms, microorganisms, and other members of this incredible underground community. Build up your soil so it's healthy and strong. High-quality soil is like money in the bank—you can draw from it for years to come in the form of delicious, healthy produce that you know is free from harmful toxins.

✔ *Make Your Own Compost*

Compost is one of nature's best mulches and soil amendments. Best of all, you can make your own without spending a cent. Compost is such an important part of the natural cycle in gardening that the whole next chapter goes into detail about how to do it . . . the *easy* way, of course.

CHAPTER 12

GREEN YOUR COMPOST

It was 1986, and Heidi and I weren't really looking for a lot to build on, but the real-estate agent said it was a great buy for California, especially here in Laguna Beach. My first reaction when I saw it was, *Yes! It faces south!* That was all I needed. Sure it had some challenges: It was basically a big hole in the ground barren of anything except a few weeds. And the soil was hard-packed clay. While I was walking around the lot, however, a vision of a beautiful home nestled into the side of the

123

hill's slope appeared in my mind's eye. We took a deep breath and went for it.

After escrow closed, the first thing I did was contact a local tree trimmer and ask to have a load of tree-trimming mulch delivered. He had two different choppers and recommended the finer mulch from a load of eucalyptus they were scheduled to trim the next week. He was grateful to save a trip hauling it to the green-waste landfill, and I was thrilled to get all that mulch for free—a real win-win for both of us. My hope was that the leaves would do what they do naturally on the forest floor: decompose back into the earth, eventually breaking up the clay and making the soil richer.

One full truck didn't sound like a lot, but when it arrived I could see that it was way more than I'd imagined. I made a good little dent in the pile the first day but decided to stop and take the weekend off. On Sunday, I went over to do some more on-site designing of the house plans, and that's when the fire truck arrived.

I knew that compost could get hot, but I'd never heard of a pile of chopped leaves steaming. I thought it was kind of funny, but the firefighters weren't laughing. With shovels and pitchforks, we opened up the center of the pile where the steam was coming from. The rising steam turned into a solid smoky cloud as fresh air touched the hot center of the pile, but a good dousing of water put a stop to the whole mess. The fire department was very clear: the pile had to be gone by the next day—*period!*

It took four of us the whole next day to spread the mulch out and cover all the weeds and bare spots about six inches deep. As I look back, that was probably one of the best investments I've ever made. Six months later, we needed another load of mulch. We went with a half load of pine trimmings to get some different nutrients, and this time, we had a crew standing by with rakes in hand. The first batch of mulch had mostly decomposed already. And when you pushed the leaves aside, where there once was hardpan soil, there was now the start of beautiful black rich earth.

We still get a load or two a year for our walkways, and all of our kitchen scraps go into compost bins that seasonally get dumped under the fruit trees. There are lots of ready-made compost bins available that make it pretty easy to "do compost" and keep your green waste out of a landfill. One company, Nature Mill, makes an automated indoor composter that has no smell. As Dr. Bill, a friend who knows permaculture, says, "Putting down dead leaves, plants, and limbs is making a deposit into your carbon savings account, just like making a deposit into your bank account. And you're making a withdrawal from your carbon account with every piece of produce you harvest."

I don't know the science of composting. I only know that our oranges and guavas are a lot happier when we compost. It's another one of those wonderful miracles of life—dead plants transforming into black compost and then becoming alive again in the fruit and vegetables we harvest and eat.

Make Green Easy

✓ *Six Reasons to Compost*

1. A full 50 percent of all municipal solid waste in our landfills is composed of food and paper.[1]

And according to the U.S. Environmental Protection Agency, food waste is the number one least-recycled material. Even though it can decompose naturally, landfill waste is compressed tightly with heavy bulldozers and earthmovers so that very little oxygen can get in to allow decomposition. Because of this, even biodegradable waste can remain embalmed for centuries to come.

2. Landfills create methane gas, a greenhouse gas that's 21 times more potent than carbon dioxide (according to the EPA).[2] Some forward-thinking municipalities are harvesting the methane gas and using it to create heat or electricity, but most landfills let it escape into the atmosphere.

3. Our landfills are becoming *land-fulls.* We're running out of open space for landfills that are reasonably close to population centers.

4. Trash is being shipped or trucked to poorer regions and to countries where it's often dumped into the ocean.

5. Landfill costs are skyrocketing, which means higher fees (or taxes) for everyone.

6. When we dump food waste, we're removing those nutrients from the food chain, requiring farmers and gardeners to purchase alternative fertilizers. Most commercial fertilizers are made from natural gas, which is a finite resource. By composting, we're creating a sustainable full circle that puts nutrients back where they belong—in our gardens.

✓ *Where to Place a Compost Bin*

Place your compost bin on a level, well-drained site where it will receive a good amount of sun each day. This will allow any excess water to be absorbed by the earth, and the sun will help in "cooking" the compost, which speeds the process along.

✓ *Recycled-Palette Compost Bin*

If you have the room and can embrace the rustic aesthetics, four recycled-wooden shipping palettes can make a great compost bin. Simply screw the palettes together standing up on their edges in order to form the sides of a box that's open on top. Be forewarned: open bins are susceptible to critters. You could make a hinged lid from scrap plywood to critter-proof it.

✓ *Trash-Can Bin*

An old plastic or metal trash can and lid that have seen better days make a great compost bin. Simply cut off the bottom with a knife or tin snips (wear gloves). There's no need to be neat. Bury the can a foot or two into the ground and voilà—you have a critter-proof bin. You can cut some one-inch holes in the side for better air circulation if you'd like, but it's not necessary.

✓*Ready-Made Compost Containers*

The Website **www.composter.com** carries more than 45 different composters. Another site, **www.naturemill.com**, has an electric-model composter for indoor use. It does use electricity and has a motor that won't last forever, but it could be a good match for those living in apartments or in urban areas without land nearby.

✓*Easy Compost Recipe*

Mix dry brown vegetation (leaves, twigs, cardboard egg crates, and even old paper) with equal parts of green waste. Greens may include vegetable scraps, fruit, plant clippings, and grass cuttings. Greens decompose quickly and provide important nitrogen and moisture. Remember that composting is an art, not a science.

What not to compost: Do not add meat, bones, dairy products, diseased plants, and definitely no dog poop, cat litter, or diapers in your compost bin.

✓*Over-Engineering Your Compost*

Some people think that making compost is like making lasagna, with carefully measured layers of green and brown creating a beautiful compost. No, it's a natural process that likes to be all messy and organic just like nature. Add an armful of green, an armful of brown, maybe a little water (depending on how it looks), mix it up, and let it be.

✓Lawn-Clipping Compost

When you mow your lawn, don't think that you can pile up the clippings all by themselves and then have great compost. Remember, you're replicating the forest. You need to mix green and dry materials in a compost salad.

Green Bite

America's 50 million or so lawn mowers burn through 800 million gallons of gas every year. That's another great reason to shrink your lawn or at least upgrade to an electric mower, if it's practical.

✓Avoid Smelly Compost

Take a walk in a lush forest and get your nose right down into the mulched earth beneath your feet. That earthy humus aroma is similar to what a good compost pile will smell like. If your compost pile stinks, something is wrong.

Odors usually signal mistakes such as trying to compost grass clippings by themselves, adding too much green waste and not enough brown, or allowing too much water to get into the pile—all of which will cause your compost to go anaerobic because it's starved for oxygen. Give it some dry brown material, mix it up real good, and that should fix things.

✔ Don't Let the Pile Get Too Dry or Too Wet

Take a look on occasion, adding water or dry material as needed. You want the compost pile slightly moist, but not wet or dry.

✔ Don't Add Lime to Compost

Some gardeners make the mistake of adding lime to their compost pile to produce compost with a balanced pH. This isn't necessary, as great compost all by itself is acid neutral.

✔ Know That There's No Quick Compost

Compost takes time, typically months or a full season. Don't assume you'll get rich black fertilizer in a couple of weeks. Have patience, and you'll reap wonderful rewards.

CHAPTER 13

GREEN YOUR RECYCLING

It was our first trip to Abadiânia, Brazil, and the poverty shocked our sensibilities and eyes. One couple in particular caught our attention. They were young, probably in their early 20s; darkly tanned from a life lived outdoors in the sun; and they stood barefoot but were always smiling. They spent their days pushing a blue wooden cart about five-feet square. It rolled on two old car tires with barely any tread. On top of the wooden frame sat what looked like a square cage of chain link and angle iron, with planks of wood above for a roof.

The couple would ply the roads, picking up plastic bottles and aluminum cans. They'd flatten their finds with their bare feet before tossing them in the cage. In the heat of the day, they'd sleep in the grass on the side of a road, using their cart for shade. At night or when it rained, they would do the same. Becky and I observed that they were providing the community with much-needed services—both trash collector and recycler.

It wasn't until the second or third time we saw them that we noticed the two toddlers playing on the pile of trash in the cage. The little girl was probably two and the boy perhaps four. I couldn't tell if they were tanned like their parents or just covered in dirt, but I suspect it was a little of both. Becky and I were so saddened to see children living a life like that.

The next day we visited a spiritual site in the village and joined hundreds of others lining up. Most of the foreign visitors wore white in respect for the local tradition. As I looked around, I spotted the young couple in line holding their two little ones in their arms. They were wearing the same clothes as the day before, as well as the same beautiful smiles that never seemed to leave their faces. Their entire focus was on their children. I don't know if I've ever seen such purposeful focus and attention. The young family was in their own world of kissing, hugging, laughing, and playing. The squeals of delight from the kids were contagious. Everyone around them was smiling with this family.

Materially, they owned hardly anything: an old cart and the clothes on their back. They had no home, no car, and no jobs by our standards. Yet here was a couple completely in love and spending every waking hour loving and playing with their children. They had a rolling playpen for them, and I was learning about what really matters in life for those who aren't blessed with a "privileged" upbringing.

Green Bite

According to the EPA, Americans throw out enough garbage every day to fill two football stadiums, yet half of this could be recycled.

Make Green Easy

✓ Shop for Pre-owned Items

An easy way to recycle is to shop for pre-owned items instead of buying new ones. It's much greener to pick up something on eBay, craigslist, or a secondhand shop. You'll save money, possibly keep an item out of the landfill, and reduce your use of *embodied energy* (all of the energy, fuel, and raw materials needed to manufacture and transport goods). Depending on where you make a purchase, you'll still use some embodied energy (for transporting the item), but it will have a far less overall impact than buying something new.

✓ Donate When You Upgrade

When you upgrade to a newer technological gadget or appliance, consider donating your older item. You might want to give it to a family member or friend who could use it. There are also organizations that collect old electronics and resell them. Charitable Recycling (**www.charitablerecycling .com**) sets up fund-raisers for charities through cell-phone recycling. At **www.earth911.org/elec tronics**, cell-phone and equipment recycling and reuse programs are searchable by zip code. Also check **www.craigslist.org** and **www.throwplace .com**, where you can list and give away items.

✓*Aluminum Cans*

Aluminum is 100 percent recyclable and can be recycled indefinitely. As a result, there are numerous opportunities for recycling aluminum cans that also raise money for good causes.

Cans for Habitat uses proceeds to help fund home building for Habitat for Humanity. Contact Patrick Kelly, Cans for Habitat program director, at 703-358-2976; or at 1525 Wilson Boulevard, Suite 600, Arlington, VA 22209.

✓*Appliance Recycling*

- **www.earth911.org**: General recycling information

- **www.epa.gov/ozone/title6/608/ disposal/household.html**: Refrigerator and freezer recycling

- **www.goodwill.org**: Accepts working appliances

- **www.recycle-steel.org**: For appliance-recycling information; or call 1-800-YES-1-CAN

✓*Batteries*

Make sure your used batteries don't go to the landfill or incinerator. Many hardware stores have battery-recycling centers that recycle all types of single-use and rechargeable batteries, including cordless-tool batteries.

Green Bite

From the lead-acid batteries in our cars to the AAs in our flashlights and the little button ones in our watches, all batteries have chemicals inside. The three most common are lead, cadmium, and mercury; and there's also a little silver, zinc, and nickel. Sending any type of battery to the landfill or incinerator means that these metals may leach into the soil or groundwater, eventually into the food chain and drinking-water supply. Play it safe, and responsibly recycle all batteries.

✓*Cardboard Boxes*

Flatten cardboard boxes and call your local nonprofit, church, or shelter to see if they can use them. You also can offer used cardboard boxes to your local **www.freecycle.org** list server or on **www.craigslist.org**. If you or an organization can collect at least 100 boxes, you can "rescue, resell, and recycle" them through **www.usedcardboard boxes.com**.

✓*CDs and DVDs*

According to the Worldwatch Institute, more than 45 tons of used CDs are sent to landfills each month. However, there are much better alternatives to just discarding them. If you're worried about personal data, you can cut CDs in half with a pair of tin snips before recycling them. At the Website **www.discsfordogs.org**, you can mail in old CDs and DVDs, and they'll be resold with 100 percent of the funds going to a local SPCA (Society for the Prevention of Cruelty to Animals).

An alternative is to send scratched CDs, DVDs, and video-game disks to **www.auraltech.com**. They'll polish them, remove scratches, and have them playing like new. You can call them at 888-454-3223.

✓*Cell Phones*

In the U.S., about 400,000 cell phones are replaced every day. Recycling cell phones reduces greenhouse-gas emissions, keeps valuable material out of landfills and incinerators, and ensures that energy-intensive materials are recycled for the highest purpose and reuse. More insights are offered online at:

- **www.wirelessfoundation.org/callto protect**: A phone-donation and recycling program that accepts all brands and models

- **www.rbrc.org/call2recycle**: Lists recycling drop-off locations in communities across the U.S. and Canada for cell phones and batteries

- **www.cellforcash.com**: Offers cash back for donating used cell phones

- **www.collectivegood.com**: Accepts cell-phone donations to benefit charities

✓ Compostable Bioplastics

The cool plasticlike disposable forks and things made from sugars and other biological ingredients are compostable only in high heat (over 400 degrees). Your home compost bin or pile won't get hot enough to break them down. You can locate a municipal composting service at **www.findacom poster.com**.

✓ Compact Fluorescent Bulbs

Many lamp manufacturers now have "take back" programs. Sylvania will take back any brand bulb: **www.sylvania.com/Recycle**. Local IKEA stores will also recycle bulbs. Go to **www.ikea. com** to find the nearest location.

green your recycling

137

✓ *Corks*

Natural-cork wine closures are 100 percent natural and renewable, but it does take some nine to ten years for the cork-oak trees to regenerate their thick bark between shearings. An alliance of concerned businesses, individuals, and ecological organizations addresses the opportunities to recycle natural cork into flooring tiles, building insulation, automotive gaskets, craft materials, soil conditioner, and sports equipment. See their Website at **www.recorkamerica.com**.

✓ *Electronics*

How about receiving cold cash for old electronics? Here are some companies that buy back your old goods and either resell or recycle them:

- **www.Gazelle.com**: Find your product and its value, sign up for a free shipping box, and receive a check or PayPal credit. Gazelle also lets sellers donate their funds to one of 23 nonprofit causes.

- **www.VenJuvo.com**: This is another site to sell or donate electronics that also lets you give your funds to a charity. VenJūvo gives users a prepaid shipping label, but customers must supply their own box.

- **www.TechForward.com**: Allows you to lock in a buyback rate in the future for appliances you purchase today.

- **www.myboneyard.com**: Accepts cell phones, laptops, desktop PCs, and flat-panel monitors; and gives Visa gift cards rather than cash.

✓ *Exercise Videos*

You can swap fitness videos with others at **www.videofitness.com**.

✓ *Eyeglasses*

The World Health Organization estimates that 25 percent of the world's population needs eyeglasses. You can help by donating glasses you no longer use, which can be reground into a new prescription. This process is offered online at **www .ehow.com/how_9169_recycle-eyeglasses.html**.

For a list of drop-off centers for old eyeglasses, you can call 800-CLEANUP. These centers collect for the organization Give the Gift of Sight, which is cosponsored by the Lions Club and LensCrafters. For additional eyeglass recycling, contact Medical Ministry International (**www.mmint .org/Resources.Eyeglass_Collecting**); or SightFirst Eyeglass Recycling Center, 34 W. Spain, Sonoma, CA 95476.

✓ *Recycling Plastics*

Recycling plastic may keep some of it out of the landfill, but it doesn't help much with their carbon footprint since recycling plastic takes almost as much energy as manufacturing it originally. Using glass or other refillables is the best environmental choice. The following lists the seven categories of plastics (identified on products by their number or name), what they're commonly used for, and whether they can be recycled. Every community is different, so make sure you know what can and can't be recycled where you live.

#1 PET (polyethylene terephthalate): *Recyclable/Safe to use.* This is the most common plastic. Two-liter soda bottles, plastic peanut-butter jars, and most household cleaning-solution containers are made of PET. It's one of the safest plastics to produce, and it can be recycled into fabrics and carpet.

#2 HDPE (high-density polyethylene): *Recyclable/Safe to use.* Detergent bottles and milk jugs are often made from HDPE. Similar to PET, this plastic is also relatively safe to produce and can be recycled. Once it's sorted, it is typically broken down into small flakes, cleaned, and reused.

#3 PVC (polyvinyl chloride): *Not Recyclable/Avoid.* PVC (vinyl) is dangerous to produce, and it leaves behind carcinogenic by-products that are often released into the environment. Shower curtains, kids' school bags, raincoats, waterproof boots, plumbing pipe, and auto interiors can all contain PVC. That new car smell is primarily the off-gassing of PVC and other plastics. Rather than recycling or tossing PVC items, call your sanitation department or environmental agency to see where a hazardous site is located. Many locations do monthly pickups.

Anne Rabe, of the Center for Health, Environment & Justice, states, "We don't recommend landfilling PVC because many PVC products contain chemicals that are heavy metals that leach into groundwater over time." According to Rabe, "Further problems can occur if there is a large fire at a landfill, which can cause PVC to release dioxins into the air."

Stop purchasing products that contain PVC, which will send a message to manufacturers who use it. Corporations including Microsoft, IKEA, Victoria's Secret, Sears, Walmart, and others are phasing out PVC.

#4 LDPE (low-density polyethylene): *Recyclable/Limit use.* LDPE is best known as the clear produce bags available at supermarkets. It's also found in dry-cleaning bags, disposable diapers, garbage bags, and drink bottles. LDPE is relatively easy to recycle, but it's better not to use it in the first place. Some cities have banned disposable plastic bags because they've been found to contribute to the demise of sea animals that mistake the bags for food.

Many communities don't recycle #4 plastic bags, but Albertsons, Safeway, Whole Foods Market, and Ralphs will accept them.

#5 PP (polypropylene): *Recyclable (but check your local recycling center)/Safe to use.* Polypropylene is used for rug backing, clothing, yogurt containers, and syrup bottles. It can be recycled and remade into other goods, but recycling #5 depends on the policy of your local recycle program.

#6 PS (polystyrene): *Recyclable (but check your local recycling center)/Avoid.* Polystyrene or

Styrofoam, as it's commonly called, is made into everything from drinking cups to packing peanuts and restaurant to-go containers. It can be recycled into building materials and other products, but when it escapes into nature, it breaks down into small pellets that are a problem for birds and marine life. It also takes centuries to completely decompose. Many cities have started banning Styrofoam, and you can, too.

Most shipping/packaging stores will accept polystyrene peanuts and other packaging materials for reuse. Cups, meat trays, and other containers that have come in contact with food are more difficult to recycle, so it's best to avoid using them.

#7 Other plastics (including polycarbonate, ABS, PPO/PPE): *Not Recyclable/Limit use.* This is the category of miscellaneous plastics with everything from Tupperware to toys. Most communities cannot recycle #7 due to challenges in reusing the materials, which are often too brittle or chemically unstable to be reused. It's best to avoid purchasing these whenever a better alternative is available. Some new bioplastics fall in this category. They can't be recycled, but are compostable under high heat.

✓ *Smoke Detectors*

The most common type of smoke detector contains a small amount of radioactive material. You can send old detectors by ground mail to the two largest detector manufacturers to ensure that they're recycled and disposed of properly.

For disposal only, send to: First Alert, Attn. Disposal, 3920 Enterprise Ct., Aurora, IL 60504. Their phone number is 800-323-9005.

American Sensors Corp. sells detectors under many different brand names and can dispose of all of them. For more information, call 800-387- 4219.

In addition, Sears stores will take back all brands of smoke detectors they sell.

✓ Sports Equipment

You can resell or trade sporting goods at a local Play It Again Sports outlet. Check out their Website: **www.playitagainsports.com** or call 800-476-9249.

✓ Tennis Shoes

One World Running will send still-wearable shoes to athletes in need in Africa, Haiti, and Latin America. Find out more at **www.oneworld running.com**.

Nike's Reuse-A-Shoe program turns old shoes into playground and athletic flooring. Information is available at **www.nikereuseashoe.com**.

✓ Used Motor Oil

Recycling information for each state in the U.S. can be found at **www.recycleoil.org**. You also can call 202-682-8000.

✓ *Recycled-Content Purchases*

Recycled-content products are made from materials that otherwise would have been trashed and hauled to landfills. More than 5,000 products have been identified as having recycled content, and this number continues to grow. (Many of the products you regularly purchase may actually contain recycled content.) Plastic lumber, recycled-glass tile, carpet, and even clothing are a few recycled-content items that have become commonplace. You can find lists of such products at **www.earth911 .org/recycling/identifying-recycled-content-products**.

CHAPTER 14

GREEN YOUR CLEANING SUPPLIES

My mother was raised on a farm in rural Mississippi where they literally lived off the land, lakes, and rivers. Her family fished, hunted, and ate what they grew in their garden. Every spring, her small community conducted a ritual of emptying out all but the heaviest pieces of furniture from their houses. The women of the families would spend the day thoroughly sweeping all the homes while the men drove to a nearby cave on the river. The floor of the cave was deep with a pure white sand. They would shovel, wheelbarrow, and truck back load after load of the dry sand.

Working together, they would cover the inside of all the homes with about a half inch of this white sand. My mother said that she detested the weeks that followed, which involved walking on the sand wherever you went. And if a bare spot would show through, she'd be the one responsible for carefully sweeping over some fresh sand to cover it.

After some time, the sand was carefully swept up and put out on garden paths or other areas in need of a little help to keep the mud down when it rained. Room by room, the wooden floors would start to reveal the beautiful wood grain below. Where previously the floors were darkened from dirt and mud being tracked in, they were now cleaned and lightly sanded. Any grease spots would also disappear, as the sand soaked up the oils.

I've never heard of anyone else using this technique. My mom has no idea where it came from or how long it had been going on, but I thought it made for a great story that shows how nature can provide a wonderful household cleaner.

Why Change Cleaning Supplies?

There are two very important reasons to change to nontoxic cleaning products: conventional products contain toxins that can be detrimental to your health, and the ways in which these products are manufactured adversely impact the environment.

The manufacturing of household chemical cleaners today creates toxic waste that is released into the environment in the form of air pollution, water pollution, or toxic waste. Not only does this come back to affect our own well-being, but it also negatively impacts every living thing on Earth. The *New York Times* reported: "Cancer rates have continued to increase every year since 1970. Brain cancer in children is up 40% in 20 years. Toxic chemicals are largely to blame."

One example of how cleaners boomerang back and bite us was shown by the California Department of Fish and Game in a test they did to determine the toxicity of common household cleaners found in waterways. Common bleach, household cleaners, laundry detergent, and dish detergent were all found in levels that are toxic to aquatic organisms. What's poisonous to fish, plants, and animals can't be good for humans either.

The other concern that everyone should be aware of is what these cleaners can do inside our homes. In so-called developed countries, we typically store all our cleaning supplies together under the kitchen sink or in a closet or laundry room. If fumes leak out and mix together, however, our homes can become a hazardous waste site. Many cleaning products contain chemicals that can react with other chemicals and create a new toxic gas or substance. For example, never mix common bleach with ammonia or even vinegar. This combination releases a potentially lethal chlorine gas.

Green Bite

"Many chemicals used in household products are volatile. . . . They can cause damage to the lungs or other organs as they are taken into the bloodstream. . . . Because indoor pollutants are not as easily dispersed or diluted as outdoor

pollutants, concentrations of toxic chemicals may be much greater indoors than outdoors. Peak concentrations of twenty toxic
compounds—some linked with cancer and
birth defects—were 200 to 500 times higher
inside some homes than outdoors, according to
an Environmental Protection Agency study."[1]

Make Green Easy

✓ Check for Warning Labels

Pull out all of your cleaning products and look
for the warning labels on the back. You'll find the
words *caution, warning,* or *danger* on most commercially made cleaners. These are required by law,
depending on the toxicity of the ingredients. Why
have potentially harmful or toxic products around
when nontoxic alternatives are available that work
just as well?

✓ Switch to Eco-Friendly Cleaners

Changing from toxic chemicals to safe, clean,
and healthy alternatives is one of the easiest green
shifts you can make. You can quickly replace all
the toxic cleaners in your home with green products; or use simple, natural ingredients or cleaners
that are much healthier for you, your family, and
the planet. The next time you go shopping, pick
up some replacements. Look for fragrance-free,
eco-friendly cleaners. You can also try some simple

alternatives using ordinary household items such as vinegar or baking soda.

✓ *Greener Cleaners*

- Seventh Generation: **www.seventh generation.com**

- Ecover: **www.ecover.com**

- Method: **www.methodhome.com**

- Eco-Building Products: BioShield dishwasher detergent at **www.eco-buildingproducts.com**

- Naturally Yours: Dishwasher detergent at **www.naturallyyoursclean.com**

- Aubrey Organics: Earth Aware household cleanser at **www.aubrey-organics.com**

- Bon Ami: Chlorine-free scrubbing cleanser at **www.bonami.com**

- Vermont Soapworks: Soap and body scrub at **www.vermontsoap.com**

Green Bite

The EPA has a "Design for the Environment" label now seen on a host of cleaning products. The label only means that the EPA has *evaluated* the ingredients and considers them to be the least harmful in their chemical class. It does *not* mean that the ingredients are safe. The weakest rat poison could potentially bear the EPA seal.

✓ White Vinegar

White vinegar is probably the most useful ingredient in any natural cleaner. Keep two spray bottles handy—one with full-strength vinegar and the other mixed with water for half strength. Here are just some of the many uses for vinegar:

Full-Strength Vinegar

- **Toilet bowl:** Remove porcelain stains by spraying, let stand, and wipe.

- **Mildew fighter:** Spray on shower walls.

- **Cutting boards:** Spray and wipe wooden boards.

- **Laundry:** Presoak colored clothes to prevent running.

- **Fabric softener:** Add ½ cup in place of fabric softener to the rinse cycle.

- **Wood floors:** Mix equal parts vinegar and olive oil.

Half-Strength Vinegar

- **Kitchen:** Clean appliances, stove tops, and counters.

- **Window cleaning:** Spray and wipe with old newspapers.

- **Carpet stains:** Spray and let stand for a couple minutes; soak up with a sponge.

✓ Baking Soda

Besides being great for absorbing odors in the refrigerator, baking soda is a natural, nontoxic cleaner that's readily available and inexpensive. (It's sold in 50-pound bags at **www.honeyville grain.com**.) Here are some basic uses:

- **Oven cleaner:** Mix a little water and baking soda to make a paste. Brush in the oven and let it stand overnight. Wear gloves and scrub it clean the next day.

- **Countertops:** Sprinkle baking soda on counters and wipe with a damp cloth. Rinse with clean water.

- **Pots and pans:** Sprinkle with baking soda, and then add a little hot water. Let soak overnight. Any burned food will come loose much easier.

- **Laundry detergent:** You can replace about half of your normal detergent with baking soda.

- **Carpet deodorizer:** Sprinkle a box or two of baking soda on carpets or rugs and let it stand overnight to absorb odors. Vacuum in the morning.

- **Grease remover:** A mix of water and baking soda can cut grease for cleaning bicycles, patio furniture, or kids' toys.

- **Silver polish:** This almost works like magic: Line a bucket with aluminum foil, and place your solid or silver-plated items on it. Add boiling water, a cup of baking soda, and a pinch of salt. Remove the silver after a few minutes to find that the tarnish is now on the aluminum foil.

- **Drain cleaner:** For a clogged drain, try this old recipe before calling the plumber or getting out a snake (the flexible metal tube you can use to push through a clog): Pour a cup of baking soda in the drain, followed by two cups of boiling water. Let stand, and see if that works. If not, add a half cup of vinegar, cover the drain, and let the mixture bubble away.

✓ *Castile Soap*

Castile soap, in liquid or bar form, is mild and can be used for all types of cleaning. In the past, it was made from olive oil, but now it may include other vegetable oils as well.

✓ *Cream of Tartar*

This common baking ingredient is a mild acid that's great for removing stains on porcelain sinks and bathtubs.

✓ *Hydrogen Peroxide*

Known for it's antibacterial qualities, hydrogen peroxide can be an asset for those who are mindful of germs. The common drug-store grade is typically 3 percent hydrogen peroxide and 97 percent water. You can get up to 35 percent strength in health-food stores, but for cleaning purposes, that isn't necessary. Stick with the 3 percent strength. Becky and I keep a spray bottle handy to use for the following purposes:

- **Disinfectant:** Wipe down counters, tabletops, phone handsets, or doorknobs.

- **Cutting boards:** After rinsing off a wooden cutting board, spray peroxide on it to kill salmonella and other bacteria.

- **Vegetable wash:** Peroxide will kill bacteria on fruits and vegetables. Spray or soak in full strength; then rinse with clean water. Research published by the *Journal of Food Science* showed effective results of using hydrogen peroxide to decontaminate apples and melons that were infected with strains of E coli.

- **Mold:** Hydrogen peroxide will kill shower mold. If you see mold inside a building, such as on a ceiling or under a window, check for a water entry somewhere, as mold needs moisture to thrive.

✓ Lemon Juice

- **Wood polish:** Mix ½ cup olive oil with ¼ cup lemon juice.

- **Garbage disposal:** Put a whole lemon down the disposal to freshen any drain odor.

- **Metal polish:** Mix lemon juice with baking soda for a paste to clean copper, brass, bronze, and aluminum (not for use on silver).

✓ Kosher Salt

Kosher salt has no additives such as iodine or anticaking ingredients. This spice of life is useful for more than just seasoning.

- **Cast iron:** Scrub dirty skillets and pots with kosher salt and olive oil. Rinse, dry well, and wipe with oil to keep from rusting.

- **Potatoes:** A handful of kosher salt will get spuds clean and seasoned at the same time.

- **Copper pots:** Cut a lemon in half and dip in kosher salt. Scrub and then rinse with water. The salt acts as a fine abrasive, and the lemon cuts grease.

✓*Always Test First*

Before cleaning with any natural method (including the tips I just included), test a small area first to make sure that products are compatible and colorfast.

✓*Oven Cleaners*

Oven and drain cleaners contain some of the harshest chemicals found in a home. Anything that says "Always use in a well-ventilated area" is telling you that it's poison. You can mix a paste of baking soda and vinegar and allow it to sit overnight. In the morning, scrub with a sponge or brush and rinse. Sure, it might take a little more elbow grease to use a healthy alternative, but you'll probably be adding years to your life by avoiding toxins while getting a little more exercise in the process.

✓*Fresh Air, Not Air Fresheners*

Most air fresheners are nothing more than synthetic fragrances that have been linked to asthma, headaches, and even depression. Open a window and let some clean fresh air in. If you're close to a freeway, try doing this in the early morning or late at night when there's less pollution from traffic.

Especially bad are the air fresheners that plug into an electric outlet. Not only are they polluting the inside of your home, they're needlessly using electricity that adds to environmental pollution from coal- or gas-burning power plants.

CHAPTER 15

GREEN YOUR FURNISHINGS, FLOORS, AND WALLS

At the ripe age of 26, I made a goal to circumnavigate the globe, carrying with me only what would fit in my backpack. Still single and free spirited, I started off across America, vagabonded through Europe, and then wound my way over to Japan where I ended up staying for six months. I found work teaching English at a private university and spent my free time studying aikido and

157

traveling the countryside. To this day I still remember the sensibilities, respect for nature, and beauty I experienced during my short stay there.

On a certain day each month, the first ones up and out on the streets were the foreigners, the *gei-genes*. This is *sodai gomi*—"big trash day," when perfectly good stereos, computers, golf clubs, and furniture are discarded to make room for newer models in millions of crowded Japanese homes. Because space is at such a premium, when a new large-ticket item is purchased and there's no place to store the old one, it's ceremoniously given away.

The *sodai gomi* after Christmas is always the best. My housemate picked up a beautiful two-year-old stereo that was wrapped in a gorgeous silk scarf. It worked perfectly.

I found a small antique mahogany table with a hidden drawer. Subtle geometric carvings decorated the side, which reminded me of Egyptian or Aztec designs I'd seen somewhere. *The designs of ancient cultures are so similar,* I thought as I carried my *gomi* under my arm back to Michiko's guesthouse—the place I resided and considered as one of the best travelers' guesthouses I've ever stayed.

Michiko's is no longer open. George, another American who was staying there, ended up marrying Michiko. They now have a beautiful, talented daughter, Saya; and George's work enables them to travel the world together. The six months or so I spent at Michiko's were some of the most fun filled that I can remember . . . but I'm digressing. Oh yes, this chapter is about furnishings.

The mahogany table was the only piece of furniture I had in my little room. It became a desk, dining table, and nightstand all rolled into one. At the end of my stay, I left it behind for another visitor to discover. Whatever I could fit in my back-pack was all I needed back then.

Make Green Easy—Furnishings

✓*Choose Durable and Repairable*

Your furniture choices are very personal. Choose wisely, and purchase items that will have a long and prosperous life. Look for styles that are well built and easily repairable. A case in point would be cabinets and furniture with plywood sides that will hold up better and be more easily repaired than cabinets of particleboard. Compare a metal file drawer to a less expensive molded plastic file drawer: the metal drawer might become dented after 40 or 50 years and maybe it will show some rust and need repainting, but it will be serviceable for much longer than the plastic one, which will eventually become brittle and crack.

✓*Buy Local, Vintage, or Pre-owned*

When you give a new home to an already made item, you save all of the energy and materials that went into making it. A restored or vintage furniture piece you find at the local bazaar, swap meet, or garage sale will have a much lower carbon footprint than even that new sustainably harvested bamboo piece that had to be shipped halfway around the world. Shipping or trucking pieces requires large amounts of cardboard boxing, foam packing, wood crating, and plastic/metal strapping, as well as all of the energy and carbon burned in transporting.

green your furnishings, floors, and walls

159

✓ *Low or No VOCs*

Keeping toxins out of the interior of your home just makes good sense in so many ways. VOCs (volatile organic compounds) are found in many paints and sealing finishes that are used on new furniture. Forward-thinking, eco-sensitive furniture manufacturers are using finishes without this toxin. Older furnishings usually have outgassed most of this nasty by-product (depending on age and finish), which is another reason to buy vintage or pre-owned. If you refinish a wood piece, look for VOC-free or ultra-low VOC paints and finishes. (For more information, see the "Safer Paints" section in this chapter.)

✓ *Be Aware of Outgassing*

That new furniture smell (just like "new car smell") is actually the outgassing of chemicals used in the manufacturing process. Petrochemical-based glues and paints are the most common culprits. Particleboard, used for a lot of the build-it-yourself modular furniture, can contain far more formaldehyde than what's healthy for your home.

Cushions that are made with petro-based foams and treated with fire-retardant chemicals are another outgasser. Look for safer substitutes such as wool batting, which is naturally flame retardant. You can also remove the synthetic foam from couch-back cushions and pillows, and restuff them with goose down. The down of old worn-out pillows is perfect for this. Also, organic goose-down pillows are even available these days.

✓ Reclaimed Wood or Certified Lumber

Wood and trees are incredibly sustainable resources when managed correctly. Unfortunately, the global appetite for all things wood is deforesting huge areas of rainforests (the lungs of the planet) each year, without replacing this critical oxygen-producing asset. If you do purchase new furniture, support manufacturers who use sustainable logging practices or wood reclaimed from a previous use, such as an old barn.

The furniture retailer IKEA has shifted to only using wood from sustainably managed forests, and the corporation is also cutting flame-retardant PBDEs and many other toxins from its products.

✓ Recycled Content

Another way in which companies are helping to lower the energy and resources used in production is by reusing materials that were already made. Recycled plastic, steel, and aluminum are the most common reused items. But you also can find recycled newspaper, cardboard, glass, and other "trash" creatively being given a new life again in furnishings, office furniture, and accessories. Further information is available on these sites:

- **www.poesisdesign.com**: Pulp-paper furniture

- **www.peterdanko.com**: Chairs and benches made from recycled aluminum

- **www.ecoloft.com**: Recycled-plastic furniture that looks great

Make Green Easy—Floors

✓*Linoleum vs. Vinyl*

True linoleum is made from linseed oil, wood flour, or cork dust over a burlap or canvas backing. It is a wonderful, natural, and durable green product. The only challenge is that there are very few companies who actually still make true linoleum products—Marmoleum being the most popular.

Vinyl flooring is imitation linoleum made from petrochemicals (including PVC). Vinyl-composition tiles are made from chips of vinyl that are pressed together under heat. Well-established health and environmental hazards have been associated with PVC, including dioxin and chlorine.

Safer and more environmentally friendly substitutes do exist. Be sure to use a nontoxic adhesive with any hard-surface flooring that must be glued down. You can check out **www.afmsafecoat.com** for safe adhesives and paints. FloorScore (**www .rfci.com**) is a certification program for hard-surface flooring and adhesives.

✓*Concrete, Tile, and Stone*

Masonry products have been used for thousands of years as finished floors because of their durability, beauty, and ease of maintenance. They also add thermal mass to the interior of a building, which helps stabilize the interior temperature.

Just a decade ago, exposed concrete was seen only in warehouses or exterior patios. Today, even the trendiest cafes and multimillion-dollar homes are utilizing the beauty of staining and sealing the concrete floors that typically exist on the ground floors of buildings built after the 1950s. If you do go with stained concrete, look for nontoxic, water-based stains and sealers.

Tile and stone are other durable masonry options. Each has its eco-advantages and impact. Stone is a limited resource and must be mined, while tile requires different amounts of energy to manufacture. High-fired porcelain tile requires much more energy, say, than traditional Saltillo pavers (named after the town in Mexico where the natural clay of the pavers is found). Saltillo pavers are sunbaked first before kiln firing. All masonry products are energy intensive and heavy to make, ship, and/or truck. So the more local the products you use, the smaller the carbon footprint.

✔ Thermal Mass

In warmer climates where concrete slabs serve as the foundation for an on-grade (earth connected) building, we see dramatic changes in indoor comfort when we pull up the carpet and either expose and stain the concrete or add tile or stone on top. Carpet and padding act as a "thermal break," separating the cool of the earth from the interior of the building. Removing this break and having a direct connection to the earth is a time-tested way for people to stay cool in the summer and take advantage of the "temperature battery" of thermal mass. Allowing the winter sun to shine in and warm the masonry floors in the winter makes this a perfect floor option for a good part of the U.S.

✓ *Wood Floors*

Wood floors have a long, rich history of lasting for generations. Solid-wood floors can be resanded and refinished numerous times. It's not uncommon for floors more than a hundred years old to still look beautiful. Today, in an effort to ease construction time and save on materials, wood floorings are being made with thin veneers over a plywood base. These can be very serviceable but probably won't last a century like solid hardwood. Be sure to check the VOC and formaldehyde level of any prefinished floors or floor finishes used.

You can find reclaimed wood flooring as well as FSC-certified wood. Bamboo makes a beautiful wood floor (even though it's actually a fast-growing grass), but most of this material is imported from Southeast Asia and carries a hefty carbon footprint to counterbalance its annually renewable benefit. Look for an online flooring supplier at **www.floor mall.com/green_flooring**.

✓ *Fake-Wood Floors*

Fake-wood floors are made under various trade names, and most are made from synthetic petroleum-based plastics, or a base of fiberboard with a plastic photograph of wood for a finish. None of these will hold up as well as solid-wood or engineered-wood floors, and they are much more toxic.

✓*Better Carpeting and Padding*

Wall-to-wall carpeting has been around only since the late 19th century. It is soft underfoot and helps deaden sound but can also harbor mold and absorb tracked-in dirt, odors, and toxins such as asphalt oil. However, it can be made from many different materials, so you should look for products that meet the minimum standards from Green Seal or Green Label Plus. Carpet pads can also differ greatly in their healthfulness for you and the planet. Petroleum-based foam pads tend to be the cheapest (little pieces of different colored foam), but they're also the most toxic. Choose better alternatives made from rubber, which meet Green Seal standards. More information is available at **www.greenfloors.com**.

Green Bite

Interface, Inc., primarily manufactures carpet squares that can be creatively mixed and matched. They offer a FLOR line that has the lowest VOC in the industry, and they recycle their products for complete cradle-to-cradle responsibility. Ray Anderson, the founder and chairman, is a visionary leader who has committed to making the corporation environmentally sustainable on a large scale. Visit the Website at **www.interfaceinc.com** or call 866-281-3567.

---

green your furnishings, floors, and walls

✔ Cork Flooring

Cork flooring is another eco-friendly option. Natural cork is a renewable resource harvested every six to nine years from cork-oak trees, located primarily in Portugal. The naturally fire-resistant material is formed into tiles and varnished for a resilient alternative to linoleum. To learn more, see **www.wicanders.com**.

✔ Recycled Glass Tile

Old beverage bottles and windows saved from landfills can be recycled and transformed into glass tiles for beautiful floor, wall, and counter tiles. Consult Bedrock Industries of Seattle, Washington, at **www.bedrockindustries.com** or call 877-283-7625. Another source is **www.sandhillind.com** of Boise, Idaho; their number is 208-345-6508.

✔ Natural Fiber Floorings

Natural-fiber floorings are similar to carpets but are made from coir (coconut husk), jute, sisal, sea grass, hemp, and other natural fibers. Some tend to shed a bit, but they're natural, nontoxic, and typically sustainably harvested; and they benefit developing communities by having a product made from their local resources. They're also biodegradable. You can research natural-fiber rugs at **www.sisalrugs.com**.

Make Green Easy—Walls

✓ Safer Paints

You can create a much safer environment for your family by painting with no or very low VOC paints. Many name brands are carrying new formulas that are better on the person doing the painting, better for your family, and better for the planet, without sacrificing the durability or performance you've become used to in paints. For VOC-free paints, adhesives, and carpet guard, visit **www.afmsafecoat.com**.

✓ Clay Paints

Low-VOC paints and even some VOC-free paints still contain synthetic ingredients. Clay paints use naturally occurring clay, which is a known odor absorber and reducer. Clay paints use soy-based resin instead of a petroleum base. See **www.greenplanetpaints.com** for more information.

✓ Clay Plasters

Clay plaster is a beautiful, breathable finish for traditional and new walls. It has a much softer and warmer feeling than paint. It can be troweled on or sprayed. There's a knack to using the product, and for high-end finishes, an expert crew is recommended. Extra clay plaster can be dried and stored to be rehydrated later if needed for patching or touch-up. This leads to no waste for the landfill. Check **www.americanclay.com**.

✓ *Milk Paints*

Traditional milk paint was the only paint option available a century ago. It has a soft look; and even though the durability isn't as good as other finishes, it's natural, safe, and can work well in areas that don't see much moisture or abuse. More information is available at **www.milkpaint.com**.

PART III

MORE GREEN FOR YOUR HOME, WORK, AND PLAY

CHAPTER 16
GREEN YOUR WORKPLACE

Becky and I had been e-mailing each other three or four times a day even though her office was in the adjacent room. It was really ridiculous for us to have two offices, which meant needing two of everything—staplers, three-hole punches, office supplies . . . you name it. I loved my private space and also had the bigger of the two rooms, but the environmentalist inside me was winning out.

"I've been thinking," I said. "How would you feel about moving our offices together?" Becky was dumbfounded. I was the one who had been most adamant in the past about needing my own "cave," yet now I wanted to share it with her. By the expression on her face, you'd think I was talking about moving to another country. But after making a list of pros and cons and doing a little bit of remodeling, we became a blended-office family. The funny thing is that we still e-mail each other almost every day—it saves on paper!

Today Becky and I, along with our two cats, live quite comfortably in a 2,200-square-foot passive-solar home/office with a 1,000-square-foot shop. Our commute is up the spiral staircase to our shared office on the top floor. Our two computers and cable TV run a lot of the time, along with the stereo, lights, and assorted appliances. However, we make more energy than we need with the 12 solar panels on our roof, which spin our meter backward. Each month we typically receive a credit of a couple dollars from our power company.

Admittedly, it's taken us three years of finetuning to get our place where it is today, which is better than *net zero* (the status earned by buildings that make all the energy they need). We've oneupped that. We're now a *positive-energy provider,* giving the electric grid our excess electrons. Here's some of what we've learned on the way.

Green Bite

Transforming workplaces in the United States into energy-efficient green buildings with better indoor air quality has the potential to generate an additional $200 billion annually in increased worker performance.[1]

Make Green Easy

✓ *Pay Bills Online*

Paying bills online saves paper, envelopes, stamps, and all the fuel to deliver the bill twice: once for the billing statement and the other trip for the payment.

✓ *Telecommute*

If your job involves a lot of time in front of a computer or on the phone, suggest telecommuting as a way to have your company reduce traffic, parking congestion, and its carbon footprint. Start with a telecommute-day experiment. Then go to one day a week, and if it works for everyone, keep on going. Working parents will really appreciate the possibilities this offers.

✓ *Be an Eco-Friendly Commuter*

A program funded by the federal government to help employees link up with local providers to find commuter rides is explained at **www.com muterchoice.com**.

✓ *Get on the Paperless Path*

The paperless office can save trees, energy, and a whole lot of storage space, as well as increase productivity. The philosophy is to use a minimal amount of paper and convert all documents to digital form. You'll need a scanner, so look for an efficient Energy Star–rated one. A possible snag you'll need to weigh is the longevity of digital—that is, will you be able to access your files in the future? Australia has started a program with the goal of having businesses cut paper use by 20 percent. See **www.projectpaperless.com.au**.

✓ *Develop a Paper-Purchasing and Use Policy*

Setting up a paper-use policy that everyone in your household supports can save money and environmental resources. Your policy will be unique to your concerns, but might include:

- Setting all printers for duplex mode to print on both sides.

- Purchasing 100 percent postconsumer paper.

- Buying tree-free paper when appropriate.

- Recycling all paper.

✓ *Kill Those Power Vampires*

Sometimes called "phantom loads" or "idle current," power vampires refer to power that's being used mainly by electronic equipment and appliances 24/7 even if it's turned off. Chapter 19 has a full description of phantom loads and how to keep them from sucking power and the associated environmental and financial expenses.

✓ Use Energy-Efficient Task Lighting

Replace those obsolete incandescent bulbs with either compact fluorescents or LEDs (light-emitting diodes). You'll save energy and also cut down on unwanted heat that's produced by traditional incandescent bulbs. And see if your lighting can be optimized to be focused just where you need it for the task at hand, instead of lighting up an entire room when you don't need to.

✓ Go for a Green Computer When You Need a New One

The U.S. has a voluntary standard for less-toxic, more-efficient, and ultimately recyclable machines known as the Electronic Product Environmental Assessment Tool (EPEAT). EPEAT helps consumers evaluate electronic products according to three tiers of environmental performance—bronze, silver, and gold. The European Union has established similar regulations, commonly referred to as the Restriction of the use of certain Hazardous Substances directive (RoHS).

✓ Recycle Old E-waste

One downside of the computer age is that computers, televisions, cell phones, fax machines, stereos, and other electronic equipment all contain hazardous materials. There are about four pounds of lead and other harmful materials in computer monitors and TVs alone. The good news is that it has become cost effective to mine e-waste for the silver, gold, and other precious metals. So recycle now rather than mine e-waste later.

Green Bite

Make sure your recycler is legitimate because a reported 50 to 80 percent of e-waste is shipped overseas or to Mexico for dismantling in conditions that pay little respect to people or the environment.[2]

In 2003, California passed the Electronic Waste Recycling Act, which makes it a felony to dispose of electronic devices in landfills and carries fines up to $25,000 per day. Fifteen other states also have e-waste laws. See **www.computertakeback.com**.

Research e-waste recyclers at **www.ease-e-waste.com** and **www.ewaste.com**.

✓*Grab a Mug*

The argument over which is better—a Styrofoam or a paper cup—is easily settled by using a durable ceramic mug. Pick up a cool secondhand one for an even lower carbon impact.

Green Bite

Styrofoam leaches a little bit of its nasty ingredients into your beverage with each use and takes about 2,000 years to decompose.

✓ Refill Ink Cartridges

That $50 printer may not be such a great deal when you find out that the individual ink cartridges cost over $20 each—unless you refill those cartridges. Cartridge World, OfficeMax, and even Walgreens will refill your cartridges at a fraction of what new ones will cost.

If you want to do your own refilling, you can buy refill kits online. It can be a bit messy, so make sure you do it over a sink, and wear gloves and old clothes just in case.

✓ Buy Recycled Ink Cartridges

Buying recycled cartridges can save 50 percent or more of the cost and eco-impact over virgin cartridges. And if you want to dispose of old ink cartridges, many Staples stores and some other office stores will recycle them and donate the proceeds to socially responsible causes.

✓ Green Packing Peanuts

Recycle packing peanuts for your own use or donate them to your local shipping store like UPS. (Most will accept them.) You can also call The Peanut Hotline at 800-828-2214 to find a peanut-recycling center near you. Check out **www.loose fillpackaging.com**.

Actually, natural popped popcorn (without the butter) makes great packing if you have to mail a breakable object and don't have any recycled peanuts on hand.

green your workplace

> ## Green Bite
> - Ink-refill kits are sold online at **www.oddparts.com**.
>
> - Recylced ink cartridges are sold at **www.cartridgeworld.org**.

✓ Think "Cradle to Cradle"

"Cradle to Cradle" is a certification for products that meet specified levels of environmentally intelligent design. It's a simple concept that requires companies to take full responsibility—physical and financial—for their products from production through end-of-life recycling, reusing, or disposal. Everything from office chairs and workstations to whiteboards is now being manufactured and certified Cradle to Cradle. See **www.c2ccertified.com**.

✓ Green Cleaners

Replace any cleaners, solvents, or solutions with nontoxic versions. If a warning label says "Harmful or fatal if swallowed," it's probably best to find a healthy alternative.

Green Bite

If you or your company contracts with a cleaning service, request that they replace toxic cleaning supplies with eco-friendly alternatives. If you meet some resistance, volunteer to supply the products yourself. For some options, see **www.seventhgeneration.com** and **www.methodhome.com**.

✓ *Stop Toxins at the Door*

Place a large, durable doormat at every exterior door to catch some of the microbes and toxins that are tracked in from pesticides, fertilizers, and residual oils on pavement and walkways. Avoid mats that shed, such as coco and sisal, which can allow soiled or contaminated fibers inside. Keep mats clean by shaking them out often.

Even better than mats is to go the way of many Asian countries and request guests or employees to leave their shoes at the door and don slippers for interior use.

CHAPTER 17
GREEN YOUR PAPER SUPPLIES

Paper has been an integral and essential part of human life for centuries. In the mid-1800s, Friedrich Keller revolutionized papermaking by developing a way to create pulp fiber by crushing wood. Prior to this, hemp, straw, and linen were the primary sources for paper throughout the world. Today more than 90 percent of paper comes from tree fiber, and almost half of all trees logged are turned into paper, with that number increasing.

Some forests are managed sustainably, but the global demand is pushing further into the last remaining natural forests, threatening the people and wildlife they support. Wood-pulp and virgin-paper products are being manufactured from clear-cut forests and shipped worldwide from South America and Asia. These biodiverse, ancient forests are then turned into single-species tree plantations, which support a fraction of the plant and wildlife species once found in those natural ecosystems.

Paper manufacturing also uses huge amounts of water and energy and releases hundreds of pollutants (including dioxin and mercury) into the air, rivers, and lakes. Sadly, many of the paper products end up in already overtaxed landfills instead of being recycled.

The good news is that recycling is on the rise, and products made from recycled or tree-free paper are becoming more available. Reducing your use and choosing eco-friendly paper products for your kitchen, bathroom, or workplace will help decrease the amount of energy and water used as well as the pollution that's produced in manufacturing. It will also lessen the amount of trash going to landfills. And the more you support the companies that make paper from recycled or tree-free sources, the faster they'll replace the forest mills that are adversely impacting the lungs of the planet and the sooner you'll see old, irresponsible behavior replaced with a renaissance of awareness and practices.

Make Green Easy

✓ *Cut Paper Use*

Recycling paper products and using recycled-content paper are great green actions, but it's even better to cut the amount of paper you use to begin with. Here are some easy paper- and money-saving ideas:

- Set printers to automatically print "duplex" to cut your paper use in half.

- Reuse the blank back of printed paper for recycled notepads or notebooks.

- Use the lightest-weight paper possible.

- Use fewer paper towels and napkins whenever possible.

✓ *Bank and Pay Bills Online*

Save paper, trees, stamps, fossil fuel, water, money, and time by banking and paying bills online. Also make sure to request online statements instead of paper ones. Some companies, such as the Vanguard Group, are even waiving annual fees for customers who receive bills and statements online.

✓ Eliminate Junk Mail

The average adult receives 41 pounds of junk mail each year. To learn about ways to reduce the amount you receive, check out **www.charity guide.org/volunteer/fifteen/junk-mail.htm**. Or pay for a service that will cut 80 to 95 percent of unwanted mail at **www.stopthejunkmail.com** or **www.41pounds.org**.

✓ Just Say No to ATM and Gas Receipts

If everyone declined the paper receipt at the ATM or gas pump, tons of paper would be saved, as well as the eco-impact that goes with it. Even some car-rental agencies and hotels are giving customers the option of going paperless. All of your transactions will show up online, and you won't have to file or trash those little slips of forest.

✓ Recycle Gift Wrap, Cards, and Paper

It's pretty easy to recycle wrapping paper for another gift, but creative types can go a whole lot further. Here are some quick and fun ideas for saving and reusing paper:

- Cut up old holiday cards for gift tags.

- Cereal boxes and paper that's blank on one side can be transformed into notepads with just a pair of scissors and a heavy-duty stapler.

- Make a scratch-pad notebook by folding five or six pieces of paper in half and stapling them together at the fold.

✓ *Learn More about Tree-Free Paper Sources*

Besides timber, there are other sources of fiber that are now being used for more environmentally sound paper production. The challenge is that some of these fiber sources are not locally available, so the transportation impact has to be weighed as well. The four sources of fiber are as follows:

1. *Agricultural waste.* Cereal grains like wheat, rice, barley, and oats are harvested, leaving behind tons of fiber-stalk waste that can be made into paper. In many parts of the world, these stalks are burned each season, adding to air pollution and CO_2 emissions.

2. *Native plants.* Bamboo, sisal, and banana leaves are being made into paper.

3. *Natural-fiber crops.* Kenaf, hemp, jute, and flax have been used for centuries for paper and clothing and offer an annually renewable source of fiber.

4. *Textile waste.* Most cotton and linen scraps are presently used for high-end specialty and art papers. This resource is limited and cannot replace wood fiber, whereas agricultural waste can. Here are some

Websites featuring good alternative papers:

- **www.livingtreepaper.com**: Flax and hemp paper with soy ink

- **www.visionpaper.com**: Kenaf paper

- **www.treefreepapers.com**: Banana-leaf paper made in Costa Rica

---

Green Bite

The Environmental Defense Fund has an on-line calculator to measure the impact of different paper choices. Check it out at **www .edf.org/papercalculator.**

✔ *Use Postconsumer-Recycled Fiber*

Recycled paper is available at every office-supply store. There's a big difference between *pre* and *post* consumer reclaimed. Preconsumer-recycled paper comes from wastepaper that has never reached the end consumer, such as scraps from the paper mill or product overruns. This is a valuable resource that's normally fed back into the paper mill anyway. A better choice is postconsumer wastepaper, which reuses wastepaper already used by customers for another purpose. This is mostly scrap paper that has been diverted from a landfill.

✓ Look for FSC-Certified Paper

Claims of recycled content are seldom verified. To be certain your paper is what you want, look for products that have the Forest Stewardship Council (FSC) 100 percent–recycled logo or the FSC Mixed Sources logo. Read more about it at **www.fsc.org**.

✓ Go Chlorine Free

Beige or brown paper typically isn't bleached. Using chlorine to bleach paper releases dioxin and furan, two known cancer-causing agents. Support companies that practice safe bleaching. Toilet paper, paper towels, coffee filters, and bulk paper are all available unbleached or bleached without the use of chlorine. Look for labels that include the following:

- *PCF (Processed chlorine free):* Contains recycled paper without chlorine or chlorine derivatives

- *TCF (Totally chlorine free):* Virgin paper with no chlorine or chlorine derivatives

- *ECF (Elemental chlorine free):* Uses chlorine dioxide or other chlorine compounds, which reduces hazardous dioxins but doesn't eliminate them

- *Enhanced ECF:* Uses hydrogen peroxide or ozone instead of chlorine

green your paper supplies

187

✓*Always Recycle*

The Living Tree Paper Company estimates that "40 percent of office paper still ends up in overburdened landfills."[1] Use both sides of paper, and then recycle it to be used again. If your community or workplace doesn't offer a recycling program yet, see about starting one. You'll be doing a good deed you can be proud of for forests to come.

Green Bite

- A paper-saving program has been started in Australia to teach businesses how to save paper and money while also being more productive. See **www.projectpaperless.com.au**.

- For recycled, tree-free, and chlorine-free paper, go to **www.conservatree .com**.

- Support corporations that want to act responsibly and assist in permanently protecting forests. Check out **www.forestethics.org**.

- Practical information about reducing paper use in offices is available at **www.eetd.lbl.gov/paper**.

CHAPTER 18

GREEN YOUR LiGHTiNG

I recently gave a presentation on going green to the city manager and some officials of a neighboring community, and when I walked into the meeting room, it was challenging to hold back a smile. The space was quite large, with tall ceilings and row after row of fluorescent lights that were all illuminated. The delicious irony was that the room had two floor-to-ceiling walls of glass with beautiful views to the outside and large wooden-plantation shutters that were tightly closed, sealing off any daylight. Only tiny slivers of sun streamed through the gaps and spaces around each louver.

This was a group of caring citizens who really wanted to go green, but they were unaware that simple choices (like letting natural sunlight in during the day) would go much further in lowering their environmental impact than what they really wanted, which was bragging rights for installing solar panels on city hall. Needless to say, I didn't tell them what they wanted to hear, the shutters stayed closed, and they'll probably get solar panels.

Each day the sun provides enough nonpolluting light to illuminate the entire planet without any help from electricity or fossil fuels. By simply allowing the natural light to come in, we can dramatically improve our carbon footprint, our electric bills, and the quality of light in a room. And there are many ways to diffuse and bounce the light so that glare isn't an issue.

We'll still need electric lighting when the sun goes down, and that's when the most efficient lighting will pay off. Changing from standard incandescent lights to energy-efficient bulbs is the simplest, most effective way to start getting in shape, electrically speaking. More than 50 percent of the electricity used in the U.S. is for lighting. Replacing one 75-watt incandescent bulb with a 15-watt CFL (compact fluorescent light) will save 60 watts of power while providing the same amount of light.

Traditional incandescent bulbs turn about 90 percent of the electricity they use into heat and only 5 to 10 percent into light. (Just try to grab and change a bulb that's been on for a while.) Fluorescents, compact fluorescents, and newer LEDs (light-emitting diodes), however, create very little heat, which means your lighting won't be adding unwanted heat inside your home or office. The interior of your building will stay cooler in the summer, and you'll be saving additional energy and money by not needing to run an air conditioner or swamp cooler as often. So conserve energy, save money, pollute less, and reduce your use of mechanical cooling in the summer—a quadruple win! It doesn't get much better than that.

The governments of Canada and Australia recently announced plans to phase out the sale of incandescent bulbs by 2012, and other "ban the bulb" efforts are taking place around the world. According to a recent report by the Washington, D.C.–based Earth Policy Institute: "A worldwide shift to CFLs would permit the closing of more than 270 coal-fired power plants. Switching to CFLs in the US alone could save the energy output of 80 power plants."[1]

Make Green Easy

✓ Tap Into Daylighting

Just as it sounds, *daylighting* means to let in the natural light of the sun during the day, which lowers the need and use for electric lighting. Numerous studies have shown that this not only saves energy, but it's also healthier because natural light helps kill mold and germs; it exercises eye muscles; and it lowers numerous disease symptoms, especially in the elderly. Business owners will be glad to know that daylighting has been found to increase worker productivity and boost retail sales up to 15 percent.[2] .

The "make green easy" goal is to install day-lighting so that you don't need electric lights during the day. Windows, skylights, solar tubes, and light shelves are all ways to bring natural light indoors.

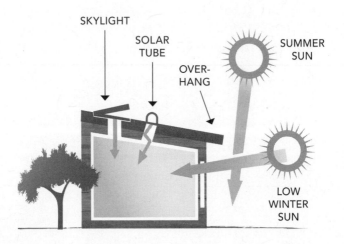

SKYLIGHT

SOLAR TUBE

OVER-HANG

SUMMER SUN

LOW WINTER SUN

✓ Overhangs and Shading

Allowing the sun's rays to shine directly onto windows and glass doors will add daylighting, but will also add heat into a building. That's great in winter when free solar heat is a blessing, but can be a real problem during summer months. Overhangs, awnings, or trellises will shade your windows to keep the direct rays of the sun out while allowing the low winter sun to enter and warm your home. For a climate-specific road map of how to use and size shading and overhangs to help with heating and cooling, visit **www.NeafLeafAmerica.com.**

✓ Solar Tubes

Solar tubes, also called light tubes or sun tubes, are small round skylights with a metallic flexible tube that funnels natural sunlight to dark spaces inside a building. They're perfect for closets, baths, and hallways where a skylight would bring in too much light. They're also ideal where the roof framing is too complicated for a skylight shaft, since solar tubes can be snaked around obstacles and, unlike skylights, require no extra structural framing.

— *Solar tubes with electric lights.* Some companies offer solar tubes that include a light fixture. These are perfect for replacing a recessed ceiling fixture. During the day you'll have natural sunlight, and at night, you can turn on the electric light inside the same solar-tube fixture.

— *Solar tubes with vent fans.* Solar tubes also come with integral vent fans for use in a bathroom. One fixture can offer all-in-one natural daylighting, an electric light, and a vent fan when you need it.

✓ Skylights

Skylights are another way to add natural light. Be sure to go with a dual-glazed model with glass that's appropriate for your climate so you won't lose too much valuable heat in winter or overheat in the summer. Single-glazed plastic or glass skylights aren't insulated well and will let heat and cool air in or out when you don't want it.

If you go with an operable skylight, you'll be able to naturally vent warm air to the exterior

green your lighting

during the summer months. An operable skylight can be opened or closed with simple extension cranks, or if the skylight is too high, a motorized electric model can be installed to work by just flipping a switch or remote control. Many buildings will enjoy a dramatic improvement in comfort and energy use with the addition of just one small operable skylight close to the highest point in the roof.

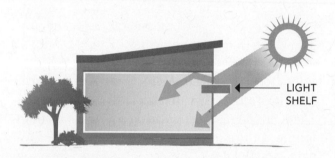

LIGHT SHELF

✓ Light Shelves

Light shelves bounce indirect light deeper into an enclosed space. They're typically used in commercial buildings, but homes can take advantage of these as well. Light shelves are installed on the inside or outside of glass windows, on the side of the building that faces the equator (south for North America). The shelves can be polished metal or a reflective light color. They shade part of the glass below, which helps in cooling, and they direct light up to the ceiling where it bounces daylight inside the building without any direct glare.

✓*Change Your Habits First*

The simplest and most effective way to save energy is to get in the habit of turning off lights when you leave a room. If you remind yourself of the connection of electricity to power plants and the environmental impact they have, you'll always remember to do so.

✓*Install Occupancy Sensors*

Bathrooms and storage rooms are great places to have occupancy sensor switches installed. These are the switches that typically have a plastic dome on them and can be programmed to stay on for a few minutes or longer. The only snag I've experienced is when the lights turned off in a public restroom, and I had to wave my arms to get them to come back on.

✓*Use Task Lighting*

Put a bright light where you need it for the task at hand and you won't need as much light to fill up the whole room. Of course for mood or romance, it's great to have dimmable general lighting, but a beeswax candle can work pretty well, too.

Green Bite

CFLs do contain a pinch of mercury—about five milligrams. (Old thermometers and amalgam fillings contained 100 times that amount.) But coal-burning power plants that make electricity for lights emit far more mercury into the air as fumes.[3] So by switching to CFLs, you'll be keeping mercury out of the atmosphere. Websites such as Earth 911 (**www .earth911.org**) and Green Lights Recycling (**www.greenlightsrecycling.com**) provide places to dispose of CFLs properly.

See **www.lamprecycle.org** for information on recycling lamps that contain mercury.

✓*Compact Fluorescent Lights (CFLs)*

The compact fluorescent bulb uses less than a third of the energy of incandescent bulbs and lasts ten times longer. If you've tried the spiral-shaped CFL bulbs in the past and didn't like them, give them another try. They've come a long way in the last few years. There's a whole new world of efficient lighting out there that offers the same color and intensity you're used to, with candelabra bases and dimmable options, too. The old incandescents are becoming a bulb of the past as more and more states and countries are banning them entirely.

✓*Light-Emitting Diodes (LEDs)*

LEDs are the newest wave of energy-efficient lighting because of their low energy use and long life, lasting from 40,000 to 80,000 hours. Fluorescent tubes typically are rated at about 30,000 hours; compact fluorescents (CFLs) at 6,000 to 25,000; and incandescent light bulbs at 1,000 to 2,000 hours. Some LEDs are a good match for replacing incandescent bulbs, especially in hard to access areas, but these little lights really shine because of their size in replacing low-voltage quartz-track lighting.

These lights do cost more up front, and low-voltage LEDs are picky about how much juice you give them. Many require a specific transformer to keep the voltage more constant. (The standard 100-volt LEDs seem fine.) LEDs are improving monthly on their brightness and color (early ones tended to be too red or blue).

LEDs are great for flashlights and battery-based systems because they extend battery life three to five times, and they have no filament to break so they're basically shockproof. LED replacements for flashlight bulbs are available at camping, hardware, and online stores.

- **www.ccrane.com**: LEDs, flashlights, and radios

- **www.theledlight.com**: LED flashlight-bulb replacements

- **www.superbrightleds.com**: LED bulbs and track-light replacements

✓ *The Color of Light*

Most lamp bulbs have a color rating on them measured in Kelvin (K). Standard incandescent bulbs that we've become used to are 2,500 to 3,000 K. Fluorescent tubes are typically 3,500 K, which is why they appear bluish.

If you want your CFLs and LEDs to match an in-candescent bulb more closely, look for those in the 2,500 to 3,000 K range. The lower the number, the warmer the light color (toward orange); the higher the number, the cooler the look (toward blue).

✓Full-Spectrum Lighting

The sun's light is considered full spectrum even though the spectrum of color changes throughout the day and season. Lighting marketed as "full spectrum" may or may not contain the full spectrum of light, as there's no industry standard. In-dividuals with Seasonal Affective Disorder (SAD) may be helped with full-spectrum lighting, but the jury is still out on any other benefits that may exist. Daylighting is always full spectrum and sea-sonally adjusted—naturally.

✓Exterior Solar Lighting

Exterior-landscape and lantern lights are avail-able with self-contained solar panels and recharge-able batteries. They're convenient where you don't have electricity or don't want to run low-voltage wires. I've found that you get what you pay for. The good ones hold up and the cheaply made and inexpensive ones don't; and unfortunately, the in-expensive solar lights end up being landfilled or taken apart for any usable pieces. Another great les-son is to purchase only well-made, durable goods that are easy to repair.

✓ *Bringing Back Our Night Sky*

Our stories of losing and finding ourselves in the stars have been told in countless poems and songs over the ages. Yet today in most metropolitan areas, we've lost the ability to see the vastness of our solar galaxy because of light pollution, which means excess light trespassing and illuminating the sky. Some cities (such as Sedona and Flagstaff in Arizona) and many state parks have passed lighting ordinances to preserve stargazing and night skies, rightly called the "ultimate cultural resource." Dark skies have been shown to benefit sea life, nocturnal animals, and of course, astronomers.

You can purchase International Dark-Sky Association (IDA)–approved fixtures to ensure that your lights are staying on your property and preserving the heavens for all to enjoy. Or consider lobbying to have your community adopt lighting ordinances that will give everyone something to watch besides television.

Check out **www.darksky.org** for more information and a list of approved fixtures.

green your lighting

CHAPTER 19

GREEN YOUR

ELECTRICITY,
ELECTRONICS,
AND APPLIANCES

One holiday season, my first wife, Heidi, and I were visiting her parents who lived near Dayton, Ohio. While we were there, under much encouragement and pleading from me, we drove for almost three hours up to Kidron, Ohio, to visit a store I'd known about for years. Lehman's Hardware is the largest hardware store serving a very select group of people: the Mennonite and Amish community.

As we exited the expressway and drove into Kidron, the countryside transformed. Rolling emerald green hills were dotted every so often with tidy clusters of barns, farmhouses, and silos. This part of Ohio is home to the largest Amish settlement in the world (not Lancaster, Pennsylvania, as many believe).

There were probably ten horse-drawn black buggies tied up at hitching posts or standing alongside the road when we pulled up to the rambling two-story barn of Lehman's Hardware. Inside, the Amish were unmistakable. The women wore bonnets and simple dresses—the men mostly straw hats and beards. The store was heaven for a tool junkie like myself—everything from specialized wood chisels for log framing to wood-burning stoves. Buggy parts were neatly organized in the two-story warehouse. I wish now that I'd had more time to just run my hands over items that I'd only read about or seen in antique stores. Here they were in brand-new, mint condition for people who still cooked on woodstoves and used treadle sewing machines.

The Amish and Mennonites are a treasure trove of knowledge. These close-knit communities have thrived since the 1600s, despite the lack of modern industrial conveniences. To this day, these old-order groups use horses for farming and transportation, wear simple homemade clothing, and have no grid electricity or telephones in their homes—a stark contrast to today's world of terabyte technology. They do use kerosene lamps, though, and some communities have allowed the use of solar electricity with batteries. But overall, they stay committed to living as they have since their founding days.

Today, I still use a lot of the kitchen and fireplace tools bought from Lehman's. They're strong, basic, and practical, just like those "plain people" moving at their own determined pace in their horse-drawn buggies. There is something appealing about their simple lifestyle, and I admire the strength of their convictions in remaining steadfast to what they believe in. These are people who opposed slavery, and they continue to object to the use of force and violence. They take time each day to be grateful for all they have.

The cost of energy used to power modern life is spiraling upward in both dollars and environmental impact, forcing increased efficiency. What most folks don't realize is that buildings in the U.S. contribute more CO_2, a greenhouse gas, to the environment than all of the cars and trucks combined. This is because the electricity used to run buildings is made primarily from coal- and gas-burning power plants. The simple act of switching to energy-efficient bulbs or turning off lights saves electricity. And every kilowatt-hour of electricity you save reduces the energy made by a coal, gas, or nuclear power plant. Every watt you conserve decreases the pollution on the planet while increasing the money in your pocket.

Going green means doing more with less, so you'll have more time, money, energy, and resources to enjoy and restore this incredible planet.

Make Green Easy—Electricity

✓ Change Power Habits First

The easiest way to save electricity, gas, or propane is to not use it in the first place. Small changes in habits all add up. When you leave a room, turn off the lights and any electronic equipment (TVs or stereos) that aren't needed. When cooking, use the smallest pot or pan that will get the job done and be sure to use a lid when you can. When your coffeemaker is done, turn the machine off and transfer your brew to a thermos or air pump. Here are more tips:

— *Dishwasher and washing machines.* Try and run only full loads whenever possible. Cold-water clothes washing is the norm in Japan and many other countries. You'll save energy, and your clothes will look better longer.

— *Refrigerator.* Set the temperature for the minimum level possible and clean off the coils below the refrigerator so it runs less often. Also, defrost items in the refrigerator instead of running them under cool water.

— *Faxes, copiers, and printers.* Your hard-working tools need their beauty rest. Put them to sleep when you don't need them, and make sure you set the mode for them to go to sleep automatically if they're not used for a bit.

✓ Stop Power Vampires

Also called phantom loads, power vampires come from electrical devices that suck electricity even when we think they're turned off. Video recorders, coffeemakers, computers, printers, television sets, and wall warts (AC adaptors) are the biggest suckers. As stated in the article "Energy Savers the Real Stars," published by The Christchurch Press: "The consumption of hidden power vampires in the U.S. is said to equal the electricity output of 17 nuclear power plants."

Here are a number of ways to stop power vampires. Choose whichever method is easiest for you to use and you'll stand a much better chance of closing your phantom leaks.

— *Unplug wall warts.* The easy way to tell if a wall wart or power cube is sucking hidden power is to touch it. If it's warm to the touch, it's using electricity 24/7, just like a leaky faucet drips water down the drain. Some items, such as cordless vacuums and razors, can simply be unplugged when you're not using them.

— *Use switched plugs.* Many rooms, especially in older homes, have an electrical outlet controlled by a switch (usually at the room entrance). Run an extension cord or power strip (that you can hide behind furniture) and plug all your appliances and wall cubes into that switched plug. When you're not using the equipment, turn it off at the wall switch.

A lamp plugged in to that same plug (with a CFL or LED bulb, of course) will be a visual reminder when your power is on.

— *Pick up some power strips.* Plug your appliances into an easily accessible power strip and simply shut off the strip when you don't need those items. This tends to work better in the garage or an industrial or loft space where aesthetics aren't an issue.

— *Check out a smart strip.* Basically a power strip with a little brain, the smart strip knows when you've shut down an appliance and cuts power to everything in the strip. These are great for computers and printers. Some even come with different colored sockets that let you keep one or two items "hot" (such as a Wi-Fi router). See **www .NewLeafAmerica.com**.

— *Monitor your power with a watt saver.* If you really want to know what that avocado green fridge in the garage is costing you each month, pick up a wattmeter. For about $30, this gadget plugs in between your appliance and the outlet. The wattmeter can tell you if your appliance has a power vampire, the monthly kilowatt use, and it will even convert that to dollars and cents. See **www.wattsaver.com**.

✓*Go with Green Power*

Many utility companies now offer green power options, which is energy supplied by renewable sources such as wind, hydro, geothermal, or solar. By signing up, you won't get the actual electrons from solar or wind electricity because utilities can't separate power that way. But you're supporting increased development of renewable energy plants, which can reduce fossil-fuel burning and nuclear power plants.

Find out if you can buy green power in your state by going to the Website at **www.eere.energy .gov/greenpower/buying/buying_power.shtml**.

✓ *Renewable Energy Credits (REC)*

Also known as green tags or tradable renewable energy certificates (TRCs), renewable energy credits are tradable commodities that represent one megawatt-hour (MWh) of renewably generated electricity. Will purchasing RECs to offset your plane trip to Paris lower any CO_2 emissions? Probably not. But buying RECs does help finance a portion of a green-energy producer's increased costs over subsidized energy forms such as nuclear power.

The U.S. national listing of RECs is available at **www.eere.energy.gov/greenpower/markets/certificates.shtml**.

Make Green Easy— Electronics and Appliances

The cost of an appliance includes two items: the initial purchase price and how much it will cost to run and repair that item over its lifetime. Newer energy- and water-saving appliances can save more than half the operating expense of models that are only a few years old. Most new appliances come with a yellow EnergyGuide label, which shows the estimated energy consumption over a year, similar to the miles per gallon of a car. The Website **www.greenerchoices.org** has an online calculator so that you can figure out the energy-savings payback comparing your existing appliance model and an Energy Star one.

✓ *Make It Last*

For centuries, it's been common for appliances or tools to be handed down from generation to generation. Now when a computer is two years old, many people start considering a new one. If an appliance is still doing its job reasonably well and with decent efficiency, do you really need an upgrade?

✓ *Consider Pre-owned Equipment*

If your computing needs don't go beyond writing letters, answering e-mail, and creating a few spreadsheets, you could easily get by with an older model. Supporting the secondhand market cuts down on the energy and resources needed to manufacture new items. A good resource for any electronic items that need a new home is eBay's **www.easytradein.com**. Also check on craigslist or even Freecycle for used electronics. Go to Target's Website (**www.target.com**) and search for "refurbished" for everything from pre-owned flat-screen TVs to iPods that have been restored.

✓ *Invest in Rechargeable Batteries*

Each year, millions of disposable batteries are used once and then mostly thrown away, with only a small percentage being recycled. Look for electronics that use standard-sized batteries (AA, C, D, 9V, and so forth), and invest in high-quality rechargeables along with a good recharging station.

Green Bite

For best results, invest in rechargeable batteries that are close to or exceeding the size of the disposable batteries you're used to. For example, typical AA alkaline disposables might be rated at 2,000 amp hrs (Ah). You can find 2,200 Ah rechargeables for about three dollars each that will match performance at only one cent a charge.

It takes only a few recycles to pay for your whole system, and many rechargeable batteries will go for 3,000 charges before tiring. Lithium-ion (Li-ion) and nickel-metal hydride (NiMH) are the most readily available replacements. Go to **www.NewLeafAmerica.com** for rechargeable batteries and chargers.

✔*Environmental Certifications for Appliances and Electronics*

There are numerous rating systems now available for appliances and electronics. Energy Star and EPEAT (Electronic Product Environmental Assessment Tool) rate aspects of the product, and Climate Counts and the Guide to Green Electronics rate the manufacturers. Comparing companies on different Websites will be a bit confusing because an individual manufacturer might rate higher on one site than another, but you can start to see the same players in the top group and others repeatedly on the bottom.

✓*Energy Star*

Energy Star is a program to promote energy efficiency. Most appliances will have a yellow EnergyGuide label that shows the annual cost of operation compared to other models.

To display the Energy Star logo, products must use less energy than standard items. Average Energy Star refrigerators need to show a savings of 15 percent over the minimum standard. Dishwashers need at least 41 percent savings, and televisions need a 30 percent savings.

Green Bite

Google projects that it will soon cost more to power a computer for four years than it does to buy one. Going with an energy-efficient model will really pay off in the future. See "The Price of Performance" by Luiz André Barroso at **www.acmqueue.com/modules.php?name= Content&pa=showpage&pid=330.**

✓*EPEAT*

EPEAT (Electronic Product Environmental Assessment Tool) is a system to help consumers compare computers and monitors based on their environmental impact. The Green Electronics Council under an EPA grant manages this system. However, it doesn't address concerns such as hazardous materials, recycling, or packaging. Go to **www.epeat .net** for lists of EPEAT-registered products.

✓*Green Guide to Electronics*

The Guide to Green Electronics is a campaign by Greenpeace to require manufacturers to remove hazardous substances from computers and take back the item at the end of its useful life and recycle or reuse it responsibly. It rates companies based on these policies. More information is available at **www.greenpeace.org/international/campaigns/ toxics/electronics/how-the-companies-line-up**.

✓*Climate Counts*

Climate Counts rates vendors of appliances and electronics on their climate-change commitments. See **www.climatecounts.org**.

✓*Computers*

When you're ready for a computer, consider a laptop. They use about half the power of a tower, and companies will be offering more and more low-power PCs in the future. Ask for one the next time you're in the market.

✓*Televisions*

Adding a full entertainment center with a large plasma screen, game boxes, and peripherals can add hundreds of dollars to your electric bills. (A 42-inch plasma TV can consume more electricity than your refrigerator.) And these megasystems create heat—lots of it—which can be a real problem in the summer. Every watt of heat made indoors needs about two watts of air conditioning to offset it. The entertainment center and air conditioner end up working against each other, using lots of unnecessary electricity in the process.

✓LCDs, Plasmas, and CRTs

If you're considering updating your older, heavy CRT (cathode-ray tube) television set to a flat panel, consider an LCD (liquid crystal display). They use only a third of the energy for the same size CRT and are 20 to 50 percent more efficient than plasma screens.

The big energy-savings variable on LCDs is how the backlight option is set. Factory settings (usually at 10) can be lowered to a less intense and more eye comfortable level (5 or 6), lowering the power use dramatically.

If you're going big and have the room, consider a rear projection microdisplay. They use about half the power for the same-sized LCD at factory settings.

And, of course, create an easy way to shut off the power, such as using a smart strip to prevent any phantom loads.

Green Bite

LCDs (TVs and computers) have virtually no EMFs (electromagnetic fields) coming off them, unlike a CRT computer or TV, which blasts up to 50,000 volts from the screen to those watching. Studies have shown that

EMFs do affect our well-being, and levels around schools and hospitals are regulated in the European Union.

✓ Stereos

Back in "the day," bigger was better when it came to stereo speakers. Those old dinosaurs may have the power to rock a city block, but you might consider donating them to a charity and picking up one of the new microsystems that are amazingly clear while using a fraction of the power.

Coupled with an iPod or MP3 player, you can enjoy the same quality of sound, and maybe those old speakers will make their way to the next great garage band that needs all that extra oomph.

✓ Rebates

Utility companies also know the benefits of energy efficiency. Because we've bought bigger TVs, more computers, and tons of electrical gadgets, many utility companies are looking at the real possibility of having to build more power plants unless we can lower consumption. To help consumers decrease their energy use, many utilities offer rebates for efficient lighting and appliances. I've found CFL bulbs on sale for less than $1 and then received a $4 rebate from my local utility for using them—that means I have new energy-efficient lighting *and* extra cash in my pocket.

green your electricity, electronics, and appliances

For a full list of rebates, the Database of State Incentives for Renewables & Efficiency (DSIRE) is a comprehensive source of information on state, local, utility, and federal rebates. You can go to **www.dsireusa.org** for a state-by-state listing of U.S. rebates.

✓ *Recycling Computers and Other E-waste*

Electronics equipment makes up 70 percent of all hazardous waste.[1] Refer to Chapter 13 ("Green Your Recycling") for information on more ways to recycle e-waste.

Staples offers electronic-waste recycling for free at any of their stores, regardless of where the product was originally bought. In addition, the Sony Take Back Recycling Program in partnership with Recycle America provides incentives for consumers to recycle their old electronics. The program includes free recycling services, discounts, and trade-up programs for consumers who recycle. Details are available at **www.computertake back.com/the_solutions/recyclers_map.cfm**. A nonprofit that links donated computers and other technology to charities, schools, and public agencies globally can be accessed at **www.cristina .org**. And information on recycling electronics, household waste, and more is available at **www .earth911.org/electronics**. Also see the "Electronics" section in Chapter 13 for ways to sell back old electronic items.

CHAPTER 20

GREEN YOUR MOBILITY, TRAVEL, AND VACATION

When I asked Becky where she wanted to go on a honeymoon, she jumped up with a piercing squeal.

"Oh, I've known this forever! I've always dreamed of riding a tandem bicycle across America with my husband."

Great. I could just imagine how much fun it would be to ride up the Rocky Mountains or through Death Valley. About a week later I asked her the same question, as if for the first time. "I told you," she said. "I want to ride across America on a tandem."

My God, she was serious. "I can't take six months off right now," I told her.

She came back with: "We could do it in stages," her excitement rising at the possibility of her romantic fantasy finally being realized.

"Let me do some research and get back to you," I said, fully wishing for a sudden case of amnesia to set in and erase that mad dream from her psyche.

We finally settled on a compromise. Becky got to pick the adventure (biking), and I got to pick the location. I went with Holland, the flattest country I knew of. The day after our wedding, with a mix of excitement and exhaustion, we landed in Schiphol Airport in Amsterdam. "The Garibaldi," our take-apart tandem and wedding present to each other, was neatly packed in a large airworthy suitcase made just for bikes.

After a few days of sightseeing, it was time to assemble our bright orange mobility machine. Putting it together at the airport was a possibility, but it would be difficult to take breaks from reading directions and finding parts without worrying about someone finding a new home for our steed. Our hotel room at the Crowne Plaza would make a much better construction site.

Our plan was to put the bike together in the room, and then make a quick escape down the elevator and out through the lobby before the hotel staff knew what had happened. Everything went smoothly. We packed the pannier bags and suited up, maneuvering our ride down the hall and into the elevator. When the elevator doors opened, my heart sank as the hotel manager and a few staff members stood there waiting. How would I explain this?

Smiles all around wasn't what I'd expected. "Oh, you're going bike touring. Have a wonderful trip. Would you like us to take your photo?" It seems riding bikes in Holland, even when exiting from a four-star hotel, is about as common as, well, driving a car in L.A. or riding the subway in New York.

The Dutch bike routes were a dream, and many hotels provided bike lockers. One of my fondest memories is of an older couple I watched make their way ever so slowly down the steps of their flat. The husband was in front with one hand holding tight to the stair rail and the other leaning hard on a cane. His wife was behind him with a hand on his shoulder for balance. At the bottom of the steps, they stopped for a moment to take in the activity, walked over to the two bikes parked next to the stoop, tossed the cane in the front basket, and smoothly pedaled off, like teenagers on a date to the malt shop.

Around the world, how we get around varies greatly. There are nearly as many options as there are cities and countries. Seeing Holland by bike was an unforgettable experience. It allowed us to take time to linger at an old windmill or slow way down and be enveloped in the fields of tulips. We agreed that riding through the fields of flowers in bloom was like floating in a rainbow. Going slow has its advantages.

> *"If you don't know where you're going,*
> *you'll wind up someplace else."*
> **— Yogi Berra**

Make Green Easy—Mobility

✓ *Walking*

If walking is an option, try it for those short trips. You may wish to add the meditation of mindful walking as a way to slow down, quiet the mind, and reconnect with nature. Simply pay attention to your breathing while you walk slowly. Don't forget to take the time to smell the roses along the way.

✓ *Bikes, Trikes, and Quadricycles*

The bicycle is the most efficient way to move people. Spending three weeks on a tandem through Holland, we saw people from ages 6 to 86 enjoying the freedom and fresh air of pedaling. Granted, the Netherlands is relatively flat, but many areas of cities and suburbia alike are bike accessible.

Trikes aren't just for kids anymore. For older individuals, the stability of large-pedal trikes can be a comfort. Large-pedal quad cars are fun for couples or even a cottage taxi business.

A few company Websites that offer human-powered options for mobility include **www.works man.com** for utility and cargo bikes since 1898; **www.lightfootcycles.com** for utility and touring trikes and quads; and **www.rhoadescar.com** for a four-wheel bicycle car.

Green Bite

Check out Rails to Trails Conservancy (**www .railstrails.org**), an organization that works with communities to preserve unused rail corridors by transforming them into bike and walking trails. A clearinghouse of information related to pedestrians and bicyclists in the U.S. can be found at **www.bicyclinginfo.org**.

✓ *Recumbent Bikes*

If you haven't been on a bike in a while and the thought of spending any time at all on a bike seat the size of your hand has you worried, check out the huge selection of recumbent bikes available today. These are the bicycles that look like you're sitting back in a reclining chair.

A recumbent bike has many advantages. You can wear regular shorts without padding because the seats are wide and comfy; they are very easy on the neck, arms, shoulders, lower back, and sit bones; and they're more aerodynamic, making for less effort.

These are serious machines. Numerous distance and speed records have been set on recumbents. Two-wheelers can be tricky to learn to stop and start, but touring three-wheelers make this much easier. Information is available on recumbent touring bikes at **www.windcheetah.com**.

Green Bite

Recumbent bikes have been around since the 1890s. In the 1930s, athletes started winning races with them, and traditional bicycle manufacturers lobbied in 1934 to have the recumbents banned from competitive events. Recumbent bicycle designs sat in mothballs until the oil crisis of the 1970s sparked a resurgence in cycling, and they've been going strong ever since.

✓ Electric Bikes

Electric motorized bicycles typically use rechargeable batteries that are charged by plugging into a standard power outlet. Electric bicycles are either powered on demand using a handlebar-mounted throttle or by pedelec (from pedal electric), where the electric motor is regulated by pedaling. Although they are nonpolluting while operating, all electric vehicles still require energy and create an impact, depending where the electricity was produced (coal, gas, hydroelectric, wind, solar, and so forth).

Many bicycle shops are now selling motorized bikes as well as conversions so you can electrify your own.

✓ Electric Scooters

Electric scooters are the big sisters to electric bicycles. They're a lot sturdier, usually faster, and have a longer range. Some can carry two passengers. The batteries are the biggest variable in range, power, and speed.

✓ *Car Sharing*

Car sharing helps people kick the car-owning habit without going cold turkey, with the financial reward of saving money. It's a club with monthly dues and reduced daily or weekly rental rates for vehicle use. The beauty is that you have the option of choosing different cars or trucks, depending on your needs at the time. Here are some Websites to check out:

- **www.autoshare.com**: Provides information on how to set up a rideshare in your community

- **www.carsharing.net**: Offers resources to reserve vehicles for city dwellers

- **www.commuterchoice.com**: Funded by the U.S. government to help employees link up with local providers to find commuter programs

- **www.erideshare.com**: A free rideshare service that connects commuters going the same way

- **www.zipcar.com**: A car-sharing company that offers rentals and partners with universities providing rentals on campuses and elsewhere

- **www.hitchsters.com**: Connects travelers so they can share taxis to and from an airport

✓ *Mass Transit*

Opting for the bus, subway, or train are other ways to get around while stepping lightly on the planet and supporting community systems that we need more of.

The nonprofit site **www.publictransportation .org** offers fact sheets, maps, locators, and ways to research the benefits of public transportation.

✓ *Neighborhood Electric Vehicles*

A Neighborhood Electric Vehicle (NEV) is a U.S. term for a speed-limited electric vehicle that won't exceed 25 to 35 miles per hour, depending on the state. These vehicles are equipped with lights, horns, and seat belts for safety on public roads. Some retirement and golf-club communities are specifically designed for NEVs or golf carts with narrower streets.

Becky and I drive a GEM car that we've fondly named "Bling" as our daily driver around town.

✓ *Biodiesel*

Biodiesel is a fuel similar to petroleum-based diesel fuel in performance, but since it's manufactured from vegetable or animal fats, it has substantially lower tailpipe emissions. Any standard diesel vehicle can run on biodiesel, but pre-1992 vehicles will need some new hoses and gaskets because solvent properties of this fuel will degrade natural rubber. Biodiesel can be 100 percent veggie-based B100 or blended with petrodiesel in different percentages of B20 to B90. The eco-impact is dependent on whether the feedstock is from a virgin source, such as soybeans, or from recycled waste oil, such as restaurant grease.

Research is being done to create biodiesel from garbage, food scraps, and even sewage sludge. These are not yet commercially available options but may hold promise in the near future. You can make your own biodiesel today from local waste oil, and even get together with a few friends and start a biodiesel co-op. See **www.homebiodie selkits.com** for automated systems.

✓ Straight Vegetable Oil

As early as 1900, diesel engines were run on peanut oil. It takes very little modification to turn a diesel vehicle into one that will run on vegetable oil. Basically, a simple system is installed that uses engine heat to thin the vegetable oil to a proper viscosity. Once your conversion is done, you can pour straight vegetable oil (SVO) or strained and cleaned waste oil into your tank and drive away.

Be sure to check on any local, state, or highway taxes.

✓ Ethanol

Running vehicles on ethanol, also called grain alcohol (the same compound found in alcoholic beverages), isn't anything new. The 1908 Model T Ford could be adapted to run on ethanol. Prohibition in the 1920s put an end to mainstream ethanol use until the recent rise in oil prices. While corn-based ethanol has been touted as a way to lower greenhouse-gas emissions and oil imports, it simply isn't a major improvement. Studies have shown that corn production in the U.S. is so reliant on oil that it takes seven barrels of oil to produce eight barrels of ethanol. And using corn-based ethanol will get fewer miles per gallon than using gas.

Agriculture waste such as straw, crops such as sugarcane and switchgrass, and even pond algae show much better promise as bases for ethanol. When these efficient ethanol alternatives are developed, we could use the new flex-fuel or multifuel cars and convert our existing internal-combustion engines to run on ethanol. Today, the majority of cars manufactured in Brazil come flex-fuel ready, capable of running on ethanol, gasoline, or a mix of both.

A small community or farm that can make its own moonshine (ethanol) using agricultural waste could produce enough fuel to meet its mobility and heating needs. Making ethanol from farm waste also looks to have a pretty good carbon footprint. The CO_2 released in burning ethanol is offset by the CO_2 absorbed by the plant during its growth cycle.

If you're interested in learning more, the best book I've found on ethanol is *Alcohol Can Be a Gas!* by David Blume.

Green Bite

For private planes, the common aviation fuel is avgas. There's already talk in the industry that avgas will eventually stop being produced or at least be difficult to come by. Ethanol is

one transition possibility. Brazil already manufactures a line of planes that runs on farm-
produced ethanol. In the U.S., an aerial dem-
onstration team, the Vanguard Squadron, has
been running their high-performance stunt
planes on 100 percent ethanol since 1993.
Converting standard sport aircraft to run
on ethanol or a combination of ethanol and
avgas takes only a few modifications.

✔ Advanced Diesel

The new generation of diesel vehicles have
come an incredibly long way in efficiency and
exhaust pollution. Newly mandated ultra-low sulphur diesel (ULSD) has an allowable sulphur content of only 15 ppm (parts per million) compared
to the previous allowance of 500 ppm. Europe has
required ULSD since 2006, and the U.S. changed
over in 2007. This has opened the door for efficient
European diesel imports to now run on American
diesel. (In the past, European autos and trucks imported to the U.S. had to be modified to handle
the higher sulphur content of U.S. fuel.)

This means that U.S. drivers can purchase
clean-burning diesel cars competitive with the
fuel mileage of a hybrid. And a diesel motor will
far outlast a gas guzzler motor in the miles you can
put on it. Both Mercedes-Benz and Volkswagen offer diesels, and many other manufacturers will be
offering diesels in the near future. This next generation of diesels will also run on biodiesel for an
even greener ride.

✓*Hybrids*

Hybrid electric vehicles (HEVs) combine a traditional fuel engine with a rechargeable battery bank for better fuel economy. Some vehicles can even convert kinetic energy back into electricity when going downhill or through regenerative braking. The Honda Insight and Toyota Prius were the first commercially available hybrids.

Hybrids cost more up front but save at the pump. An analysis by **www.intellichoice.com** showed that 22 currently available HEVs will save their owners money over a five-year period. And rebates and tax credits may be available to make hybrid purchases even more attractive.

Green Bite
Diesel hybrids show incredible promise for high mileage and reliability. Volkswagen made a prototype diesel-electric hybrid that could get 120 miles per gallon.

✓*Plug-in Hybrid Electric Vehicles*

Plug-in Hybrid Electrical Vehicles (PHEV) are basically hybrid vehicles with larger battery packs, which offer increased range. This handles the big drawback of pure electric vehicles—limited range. The fuel engine kicks in to charge the batteries when they run low. The biggest advantage with plug-ins is that they can run solely on electricity for a good part of a trip. This can translate into fuel costs of less than $1 per gallon.

PHEVs could also lower greenhouse-gas emissions considerably. Even if you charge a PHEV off the conventional grid, while it runs on gasoline it emits 40 percent less CO_2, 35 percent less carbon monoxide, and almost 50 percent fewer volatile organic compounds (VOCs) than standard internal-combustion engines, according to the National Renewable Energy Laboratory (NREL).

PHEVs also offer a revolutionary way to regulate the electric power grid and possibly lessen the need to construct more power plants. By storing excess grid power in a large amount of PHEV battery packs, and then pulling that power back onto the grid when needed during peak use times, utilities could stretch the carrying capacity of power plants. The individual PHEVs could recharge during off-peak times using cheaper power.

As of this writing, no commercial plug-ins are available, but hundreds have been created by installing bigger battery banks into standard hybrids. Auto manufacturers promise to release factory-made plug-ins very soon. Visit the Website **www .CalCars.org** to learn about a group dedicated to promoting PHEVs.

✓ Electric Vehicles

An electric vehicle (EV) uses an electric motor that runs off stored energy, usually in a battery bank. As battery and energy storage technologies improve, so will the range of electric vehicles— their only real drawback. EVs have far fewer parts than internal-combustion engines, lowering repair and maintenance visits. They can also feature regenerative braking, a standard on many hybrid vehicles that allows a significant portion of the energy to be recovered during braking or downhill runs, increasing the vehicles' efficiency and range.

Numerous smaller manufacturers offer electric vehicles ranging from small one-person transporters to electric pickup trucks or hot-rod sports cars, such as the Tesla (**www.TeslaMotors.com**) or the futuristic Aptera (**www.Aptera.com**).

✓ *Driving Better*

Since most of us drive cars with internal-combustion engines, here are some ways to increase fuel efficiency, save money, and lower your vehicle's eco-impact:

- Drive at the minimum speed limit. Driving 55 mph instead of 65 could increase your fuel mileage by 10 percent.

- Keep your car tuned up. Also, change the air and oil filters as recommended.

- Check that the tires are inflated properly. And when it's time for new ones, consider low rolling resistance tires (LRR) that can cut fuel use.

- Lighten your load. Removing any unnecessary extra weight from your vehicle will help use less fuel.

- Don't top off the tank. Squirting a little extra fuel after the pump stops lets fumes escape into the air, releasing small amounts of VOCs (volatile organic compounds).

- Put on a roof rack only when you need it. Racks can add wind drag, which affects your mileage.

- Use the air conditioning. Running your AC does impact fuel use, but at speeds above 30 mph, the increased aerodynamics from having the windows up is a better choice. A good basic rule is to roll your windows down when you're cruising around town and keep them up when you're on the freeway.

Make Green Easy— Travel and Vacation

✔ Deciding Where to Go

Before you book a flight to Paris for a long weekend getaway, check to see if something will satisfy your wanderlust that's a little closer to home. You might be surprised to find a little hideaway that's ideal for what your heart desires. And traveling less will give you more time to play. State and national parks are also a great place to chill, especially with kids in tow.

Search for a vacation by event (cycling, rafting, and so on) or by location at **www.sustainabletravelinternational.org**. Or visit **www.rainforest-alliance.org** for sustainable tourism options. The site **www.unep.fr/greenpassport** offers a U.N. program with great information on sustainable tourism that's good for the local economy, the local community, and the planet.

✓ Experience Nature

"Look deep into nature, and then you will understand everything better."
— **Albert Einstein**

Entertain the possibility of experiencing different natural systems, such as a desert, river, lake, ocean, or forest. You can create a holiday by camping under the stars or finding a four-star lodge with all the amenities. Either way, you'll be rewarded with the added bonus of nature's regenerative, healing, and inspirational effects.

Green Bite

According to recent findings, "Spending time in 'green' settings reduced ADHD symptoms in a national study of children aged 5 to 18." The study was conducted by Frances Kuo, Ph.D., and Andrea Faber Taylor, Ph.D., of the University of Illinois at Urbana-Champaign.

✓ How to Get There

How you get from point A to point B can be another opportunity to stretch your green lifestyle. There are so many options, with commercial aircraft probably at the top of the carbon-impact list. Have fun and explore other possibilities, such as a sailboat or a bus trip, to white-water rafting or overland exploring on horseback. Budget travel is also available. Check out the opportunities at Green Tortoise Adventure Travel (**www.green tortoise.com**).

✔ *Try the Train*

It might take more time to travel by train, but you'll see more of the countryside, avoid the hassle of airport security, and feel good about contributing fewer greenhouse-gas emissions. Rail travel uses less fuel per passenger mile than cars or commercial airlines. One study showed that passengers who fly from London to Paris to Brussels generate ten times more carbon dioxide than travelers who go by rail.[1]

Most continents have very good rail service; and some countries, like Japan with its bullet trains, are wonderful. Major U.S. cities, including San Francisco and Washington, D.C., offer abundant routes. Smaller regions are challenged and will need improvement as we transition to different energy sources.

✔ *Driving Lightly*

Rather than put miles on your own car, rent a hybrid electric vehicle or efficient diesel car that you can even fill up with biodiesel at a station such as SeQuential in Oregon. Go to **www.evren tal.com** to find hybrid-electric cars at eight locations along the West Coast of the U.S. Try

www.bio-beetle.com for rentals of Volkswagens fueled with biodiesel available in Maui, Hawaii.

✓*Find a Green Hotel*

One way to make your vacation greener and healthier is to choose a hotel that's committed to bettering its environmental footprint. Eco-resorts are available in most tourist destinations, and even major hotel chains are doing green makeovers. Help move green into more hotels by patronizing those that match your environmental ethic. Check out these Websites:

- **www.ethicaltraveler.org**: A grassroots alliance uniting adventurers, tourists, travel agencies, and outfitters

- **www.environmentallyfriendlyhotels .com**: Rates properties worldwide in seven areas on a point system, depending on hotels' eco-friendly commitment

- **www.responsibletravel.com**: Displays handpicked holidays from global-tour operators

- **www.rezhub.com**: Helps you find a hybrid vehicle and book a green hotel

✓*During Your Stay*

A great way to see the local sights, once you've arrived, is to walk or rent a bike. Also, let housekeeping know that you're okay with keeping your same sheets or towels for a few days. (Most hotels will have signs you can hang out.) Bring a reusable water bottle for everyone in your group.

✓ *Carbon Offsets*

Carbon offsets are a way to lower environmental impact (of, say, your plane trip to your destination) by investing money in companies that plant trees, help build wind farms, or develop energy-saving projects; basically, it's paying for emission reductions to take place somewhere so that it offsets your own emissions.

It's much better to lower your own personal carbon footprint first, and then look at supporting sustainable projects that sequester carbon responsibly in other parts of the world. Be sure to check the credibility of the carbon-offset fund you want to support.

Carbon-footprint calculators are available at **www.carboncounter.org**, **www.carbonfootprint .com**, and **www.safeclimate.net**. You can research carbon-trading companies at **www.terrapass.com** and **www.nativeenergy.com**.

Green Bite

Beware of unethical or misleading practices. Carbon trading has been sold for projects that would take place anyway, and some carbon-offset tree-planting projects have removed biologically rich forests and planted

---

| green your mobility, travel, and vacation

nonnative single-species farms. Research all carbon-trading credits you support to make sure that they're helping to fund true environmental solutions.

SMALL STEPS— HUGE SHiFT

"The problem will not be solved by the same minds that created it."
— **Albert Einstein**

This book was written to help answer the questions I'm most often asked, but early on a more important message emerged—one that empowers and asks each of us to join together in partnership as part of a peaceful global revolution that is unfolding.

On our planet right now, more than a million environmental and humanitarian organizations are actively doing the work of restoration and healing, all without a single leader. This revolution of consciousness is a revolving *away* from what has proven to be compromising to the natural systems that we rely upon for our life support, and a revolving *toward* a deep remembering and embrace of living in harmony with the natural orders of the universe on this incredible oasis we call Earth.

As we go forward, our consciousness is being raised and our collective choices are changing. We're finally realizing that it's far easier to work with nature than against her. In the past, science has been so proud to proclaim many a project as "a modern feat of science, a triumph over nature." My hope is that this claim has ceased to be a subject of pride. It is nature that must thrive in order for us, as a part of her, to also thrive within her care. Whatever we appreciate—will appreciate.

Each of us is adding a spice or flavor to the cosmic soup of this next age with every thought and action we take. Our awareness of the interconnection and interdependence to all of life is becoming more obvious and real. It has been proven by both the biosphere project and the space station that we cannot survive without our connection to the lush, intertwined biodiversity of creation. Humans can't begin to scratch the surface of replicating the vast diversity of life-forms that the Source of this universe has placed here, interdependent on each other for individual and total survival of the whole of nature.

Earthworms and other organisms digest waste and make the soil fertile for plant growth. Plants depend on birds, bees, and butterflies for pollination of their flowers and fruits. Animals and humans depend on plants for the oxygen they provide through photosynthesis. Plants also provide shelter and food for many animals, including humans. Plants, animals, and humans depend on the sun, rain, and soil for all of our basic needs. All life on this planet depends on one another to thrive. The green movement is a raising of our awareness and consciousness so that we make choices that are respectful and restorative of life.

We're moving toward a postpetroleum world, a time when the furnishings in our home and the food in our fridge can be chosen with a heartfelt knowing that seldom touches us as we shop in today's malls and grocery stores. But attempting to slip passively into this new way of living will not work. Our choices, of necessity, must be active decisions to return to a wisdom of how to interact with an incredible and bountiful environment that itself has been created to support us through any and all transitions we can imagine. If that wisdom seems new and different to us, it's only because we've forgotten that nature is a nurturing mother who continuously offers to support us fully, if only we in turn acknowledge and utilize her potential.

The changes to come in our lives don't have to be overwhelming. We can make small changes incrementally, one little choice at a time—a different lightbulb, a purer shampoo, fair-trade coffee, a reusable water bottle. Each suggestion in this book is but one possible footprint on an emerging pathway that will lead to the lives of our children and grandchildren for generations to come. But as the ancient proverb advises, "Every journey begins with a single step."

The shift to come, in contrast to our individual steps, looms as huge and will remold all our ways of living. The impact, if we're awake enough to begin making constant conscious decisions about our lives and activities, can be—in a word— magnificent. It's a return to a more natural presence in our daily existence, an elimination of so much that has affected and still affects the world in a negative manner. Our mission, in essence, is to see the possibilities available to us every day and then act on those possibilities.

Even if humans could continue to use fossil fuel or natural resources for another 50 years in the way we have and at the rate we do now, would we really want the environmental impact that would result from that? And what's the worst thing that could happen if we transition to better energy efficiency, more conscientious environmental stewardship, and clean renewable energies? Well, let's see. We'll have a healthier planet with more plant and animal species, cleaner air and water, and improved health, all while slowing down the amount of greenhouse gases we emit. What could be the worst thing that happens if we *don't* collectively start the transition now? That's a scenario I'd rather not focus on. It does seem clear that going green is by far the most inspired and sane of the two choices on the table.

New York Times columnist Thomas Friedman wrote: "It is so much more important to change your leaders than change your light bulbs." For me, the answers to the global environmental and social challenges must include both: inspired leadership *and* better choices. As Walmart's Lee Scott said, "We will not be measured by our aspirations. We will be measured by our actions." My intention is that you will be so inspired by the green movement that you become a leader in your family, workplace, and neighborhood—or even in your city, state, or country.

Together we can imagine and then create individuals, households, communities, cities, and nations that gracefully make the transition into a thriving future that is in harmony with the spirit of life and the spirit of the planet. We don't know all the answers or how the mystery of the future will unfold. But when I look around at the power of the sun, the teeming life in our oceans and forests, or the miracle of a newborn, I can't help but see a benevolent universe that wants only our highest good.

Take a few small steps today and initiate the changes you desire. Bring others along and grow your community. But most important, enjoy the ride. It's going to be an incredible one.

This new transition has the potential to be the most exciting time humanity has ever experienced —when we collectively face the opportunity to reinvent what it means to live in true harmony with this incredible planet and, just as vital, with each other. Gandhi may have said it best: "We must be the change we wish to see in the world."

ENDNOTES

Introduction: The Big Green Picture

1. U.S. Army Corps of Engineers, April 2007.
   www.theoildrum.com

Chapter 1: Busting Green Myths

1. www.cleanair.org

2. www.timesonline.co.uk/tol/news/uk/science/
   article2195538.ece

3. Carbon footprint definition,
   www.wikipedia.org

4. U.S. Environmental Protection Agency,
   www.epa.gov

5. www.nytimes.com/2008/01/27/realestate/
   commercial

Chapter 3: Green Your Personal-Care Products

1. Environmental Working Group, www
   .cosmeticsdatabase.com

2. www.naturemoms.com

3. CancerIQ, www.canceriq.org

4. U.S. Food and Drug Administration, www.fda.gov

5. www.thegreenguide.com

Chapter 5: Green What You Eat

1. www.srb.stanford.edu

2. www.worldwatch.org

3. www.infowars.com/articles/science/bees_
organic_bees_are_thriving.htm

4. www.fao.org/ag/magazine/0612sp1.htm

5. www.en.wikipedia.org/wiki/vegetarian

6. www.en.wikipedia.org/wiki/environmental_
effects_of_meat_production

7. www.worldwatch.org/node/1626

8. www.dotearth.blogs.nytimes.com/2008/04/11

9. www.commondreams.org/views07/0120-20.htm

10. www.gsmcweb.com

11. www.fda.gov/cvm/documents/barlam_text.htm

12. www.thecampaign.org

13. www.bbs.chinadaily.com.cn/viewthread
.php?action=printable&tid=508717

Chapter 6: Green Coffee and Tea

1. www.globalexchange.org/campaigns/fair
trade/3563

2. www.treehugger.com/files/2004/11/ecotip_
coffee_c.php

3. www.osha.gov/SLTC/styrene/recognition.html

Chapter 8: Green Your Pets

1. www.sundancechannel.com/blogs/tree hugger/390257246

2. www.thegreenergrass.org/labels/interviews.html

3. www.healthyhappydogs.com/apiarticle

4. www.nrdc.org/health/effects/pets/execsum.asp

5. www.petproductskill.com

6. http://newanimalcontrol.org/wastetogas.shtml

7. www.grist.org/advice/ask/2005/09/26/kittylitter

Chapter 10: Green Your Water

1. www.energy.ca.gov/2005publications

2. www.earthpolicy.org

3. www.ciwmb.ca.gov/condemo/shingles

4. www.epa.gov/nps/toolbox/surveys/lake champlainsummary.pdf

5. www.mistercarwash.com/faq.aspx

Chapter 12: Green Your Compost

1. www.nsassessment.ca/nse/waste/docs

2. www.epa.gov/methane/scientific.html

Chapter 14: Green Your Cleaning Supplies

1. www.preventcancer.com/work/home/ carcinogens_home.htm

Chapter 16: Green Your Workplace

1. Commission for Environmental Cooperation (CEC), *Green Building in North America: Opportunities and Challenges*

2. Basel Action Network and Silicon Valley Toxics Coalition report *High-Tech Toxic Trash from USA Found to Be Flooding Asia.* **www.ban.org/ban_news/ewastepr.html**

Chapter 17: Green Your Paper Supplies

1. **www.livingtreepaper.com**

Chapter 18: Green Your Lighting

1. **www.nmenv.state.nm.us/swb/doc/fluorescent.html**

2. **www.cityofseattle.net/light/conserve/sustainability/studies/cv5_ss.htm**

3. **www.treehugger.com/files/2007/03/mercury_in_ener.php**

Chapter 19: Green Your Electricity, Electronics, and Appliances

1. **www.en.wikipedia.org/wiki/e-waste**

Chapter 20: Green Your Mobility, Travel, and Vacation

1. **http://www.eurostar.com/UK/us/leisure/about_eurostar/environment/greener_than_flying.jsp**

ACKNOWLEDGMENTS

*"The bird a nest, the spider a web,
man friendship."*
— **William Blake**

With deep gratitude for inspiration, encouragement, and help along the way: Ann Prelitz, Becky Prelitz, Roger Montgomery, Theresa Cordova, Ron Roth, Doreen Virtue, Steven Farmer, Kevin and Janet Buck, Michelle Spieker, Olga Epelman, Scott and Suzie Weber, David Bainbridge, David Eisenberg, Motts and Judy, Bucky, Amory B. Lovins, Albert Bates, Rob Hopkins, Richard Heinberg, James Lovelock, Edward Mazria, Turko Semmes, Ken Haggard and Polly Cooper, Esther and Jerry Hicks, and Harald N. Rostvik.

For artwork, editing, and publication: Gregory and Amy Rose Grigoriou, Christy Salinas, Jill Kramer, Lisa Mitchell, Stacey Smith, Reid Tracy, and everyone involved at Hay House.

245

Some have passed on and are still with me in thought and inspiration: Heidi, Dad, Grandpa, Dirck Prelitz, David Nuuhiwa, Nader Kahlili, Neise, and Deborah.

ABOUT THE
AUTHOR

Chris Prelitz was raised in the diverse traditions of his ocean- and aerospace-engineer father and his mother of Native American descent. Growing up in the midst of these two extreme views of life provided him with an appreciation for both high-tech and indigenous principles that have stood the test of time yet have been mostly forgotten. Chris is a pioneer of the green movement, heading a successful design-build firm with projects ranging from off-grid solar ranches to a green Mercedes-Benz showroom, the first solar auto dealership in the U.S. Chris now touches audiences globally with his uplifting green message, appearing regularly in print and broadcast media, including the premier episode of the Discovery Channel's *Greenovate* show.

Chris has been passionately dedicated to green living and sustainability for more than 25 years. He and his wife, Becky, share a green solar-powered home that he designed and built in Laguna Beach, California. Most months they produce more energy than they use and receive a credit from their power company instead of a bill. Chris can be contacted at **www.NewLeafAmerica.com** or **www. Prelitz.com.**

We hope you enjoyed this Hay House book. If you'd like to receive a free catalog featuring additional Hay House books and products, or if you'd like information about the Hay Foundation, please contact:

Hay House, Inc.
P.O. Box 5100
Carlsbad, CA 92018-5100

(760) 431-7695 or **(800) 654-5126**
(760) 431-6948 (fax) or **(800) 650-5115 (fax)**
www.hayhouse.com® • **www.hayfoundation.org**

Published and distributed in Australia by:
Hay House Australia Pty. Ltd., 18/36 Ralph St., Alexandria NSW 2015 • *Phone:* 612-9669-4299 • *Fax:* 612-9669-4144
www.hayhouse.com.au

Published and distributed in the United Kingdom by:
Hay House UK, Ltd., 292B Kensal Rd., London W10 5BE
Phone: 44-20-8962-1230 • *Fax:* 44-20-8962-1239
www.hayhouse.co.uk

Published and distributed in the Republic of South Africa by:
Hay House SA (Pty), Ltd., P.O. Box 990, Witkoppen 2068
Phone/Fax: 27-11-467-8904 • orders@psdprom.co.za
www.hayhouse.co.za

Published in India by: Hay House Publishers India, Muskaan Complex, Plot No. 3, B-2, Vasant Kunj, New Delhi 110 070
Phone: 91-11-4176-1620 • *Fax:* 91-11-4176-1630
www.hayhouse.co.in

Distributed in Canada by:
Raincoast, 9050 Shaughnessy St., Vancouver, B.C. V6P 6E5
Phone: (604) 323-7100 • *Fax:* (604) 323-2600
www.raincoast.com

Tune in to **HayHouseRadio.com®** for the best in inspirational talk radio featuring top Hay House authors! And, sign up via the Hay House USA Website to receive the Hay House online newsletter and stay informed about what's going on with your favorite authors. You'll receive bimonthly announcements about Discounts and Offers, Special Events, Product Highlights, Free Excerpts, Giveaways, and more!
www.hayhouse.com®